How to Make Money selling chocolates
By Matthew Short

How to Make Money Selling Chocolates by Matthew Short

Books may be purchased by contacting the author at:

www.lickthespoon.co.uk

Cover Design: Lick the Spoon
Interior Design: Lick the Spoon
Publisher: Amazon
Editor: Diana Short
ISBN: 9781521849996

Photographic credits: Thank you to Matthew Short, Diana Short, Tina Ingamells, Michael Holman – Red Forge Studios
First Edition

Dedication

For my wife and founder of Lick the Spoon Diana Short, without whom this journey wouldn't have been possible, and my children Harrison and Thomas who have shared so much of this journey.

Table of Contents

5

Introduction

Opening and running a chocolate shop can be exciting, fulfilling and for many people the chance to live their dream job. The opportunity to be your own boss is a compelling one, and as a chocolate shop owner delighting your customers with the "Food of the Gods" what's not to like?

Then you wake up at 4 o'clock in the morning with a cold sweat. You're about to plough your entire life's savings plus some money borrowed from family and friends, and if you're lucky a loan from the bank, into your new venture. But are you doing the right thing, will it make you money and serve your lifestyle or will it be a bottomless money pit dragging your spirit down?

We were in this very position in September 2009. We had been running a chocolate making business from home for two and a half years with some critical and financial success, but not enough to support us as a family.

We wanted to take the next step to what we thought would be a 'proper' business - a production facility and a chocolate shop. The next seven years can only be described as the proverbial roller coaster ride!

We remortgaged our house opened a chocolate factory and a chocolate shop. Ran the shop for five years and won multiple awards before selling it at a profit. We opened three pop up shops attended food fairs everywhere from our local schools to London's Olympia and continue to win awards and supply the most highly renowned luxury stores and chocolate shops throughout the UK and Ireland.

But we made a lot of mistakes on the way and at one point were a few weeks away from bankruptcy! So in this book we'll give you the benefit of those mistakes, without the associated costs, and our consequent best advice on opening and running a chocolate shop and cafe.

The comprehensive information given in this book might be applied to any small retail business.

We'll talk about everything from business plans to finding a premises. How to run a pop up shop on a shoe string budget and the pros and cons of buying or leasing a premises. We'll discuss environmental health implications and the practical elements of branding and fitting out a shop.

When you finish this book you'll effectively have 10 years experience and will have all the information to allow you to open and run a successful and profitable retail business!

We won't tell you how to make chocolates or set up and run a chocolate factory – that's another story!

If before embarking on your journey you'd like to know more about how chocolate is made please read appendix 2 first. If you'd like to know a brief history of the chocolate shop then please read appendix 3. But if you can't wait to get started dive into the next chapter!

1: BBC One Show filming in our chocolate shop with presenter, author and food critic Jay Rayner

Planning your business

Why are you starting a business?

This might seem like simple question but it is key to plotting your way forward.

A change of lifestyle and the chance to control your destiny, be your own boss are often the driving reasons to start a business, but unless you have no mortgage, no bills and are fully self sufficient, you will want to do more than break even. (..and if you are in the above position, what are you thinking?! Get back to your armchair and enjoy the sunset!)

Harsh truth #1 -Becoming your own boss may sound like a fantastic idea but the truth is you'll be working for a mad person!

Not only will you have to do the things you like doing - perhaps conversing with your customers as the benevolent patron or creating mouthwatering confections in a flurry of cocoa powder and a "Vianne Rocher"1950's headscarf but you'll also need to find time to do the accounts, payroll, Human Resources, Marketing, Ordering, Stock Control, Cleaning.... you get the picture!

To start your business you'll probably be making a significant financial investment of your own money and possibly that of family, friends, the bank or even crowd funding. You'll also stand a chance of burning through a significant amount of cash in the early days once your business has opened.

So let's assume you aim to make money, you just need to decide how much. Easy. You're potentially going from a position of financial security to one of high financial risk. So how much money does your business need to make to be worth that risk, or how much will your lifestyle change to make the risk worth it?

REALITY CHECK Decide at the start why you really want to open a shop - is it to grow your wealth or for a change of lifestyle?

What do you want to achieve – money – how much?

If you're a starting a business to try and earn more money than you could in your existing job, it's worth taking stock of your current income and associated security. Write it down...and not just the salary, but the paid holidays, the pension, the subsidised canteen lunches, the free cups of coffee, the pilfered biros, the paid sick days and the gratis Christmas bash!

So how much money do you want or need your business to pay you per year? 20,000, 50,000; 200,000; a million?

Pick a figure that you'd like to achieve and write it down as your 5 year goal.

What will your business need to look like in order to generate that kind of money?

This is where it gets more difficult as you'll need to speculate. We'll break this down into more detail later to help you plan but in order to earn any amount of money, you'll need to be generating **profit** from **sales** and covering all your **costs**.

Your costs will depend on the planned size of the business – how many sites, how many staff, how many people needed to run the business?

Any small business owner will tell you that you need to wear many hats. Whether you are planning a single small shop or an ambitious chain, the required roles will still need to be allocated to someone – even if that someone is always you! As your business grows, the roles can be delegated to new staff.

The roles you identify might include...

- Sales Manager
- Production operative
- Cleaner
- Accountant
- Payroll
- Human Resources
- Operations Manager
- Marketing
- Ordering and buying
- Managing Director

TIP Decide how much money your business needs to make you and what the business looks like to achieve that

What do you want to achieve - lifestyle?

In a world where growth is the Holy grail and everyone dreams of pitching to Dragons' Den, setting out simply to maintain a lifestyle for you and your family, with perhaps a small profit at the end of the day, might seem rather unambitious.

The idea of being your own boss, able to come and go as you please and potentially give employment to family members is appealing. There is however a big, fat fly in the ointment!

REALITY CHECK There is a fundamental contradiction between a family friendly lifestyle and running a retail store alone as "owner occupier".

The times when you want relax and be with your family - at weekends, in the summer and bank holidays are the times when everybody goes shopping. Particularly so if you're in a touristic area. You're going to need to employ some reliable staff.

It would be a mistake to believe that a business does not need planning and tight management in order to achieve that perfect work life balance. Training is everything. Most people want to get things right. There's a reason that big franchises work – everybody knows what to do and they have the tools to do it. If you fail to train your staff adequately, you'll most likely be the one who opens the shop every morning and the one who cleans and cashes up at the end of the day. It'll be hard work and it will be very hard to find staff members who'll be as passionate about the business as you are.

2: *Running a retail business with a young family can be challenging but they are good at flyering!*

Running a chocolate shop is ultimately a nice thing to do. Almost everybody who visits a chocolate shop will do so because they love what you do and you'll gain many regular customers and meet new people all of the time. To make it successful you'll need to be committed to the highest service and customer satisfaction levels and that requires hard work, good organisation and great products.

We opened our own Chocolate Shop in November 2009 just one month after opening our Chocolate Factory – with hindsight a rather ambitious move! Our two children were aged 2 and 4 at the time.

Pros – somewhere to showcase and sell our products

- great brand exposure

- instant and constant market research

Cons – increased overheads

- unsociable working hours

- ultimate responsibility to stand in if staff are sick or on holiday

Why you should write a business plan

Writing a business plan is probably the first of a great number of things you might not *want* to do but absolutely should in order to make your venture successful.

Bottom line, the more you're avoiding it, the more likely it is you need one!

I've met a great number of creative, intelligent people capable of making the most glorious products, engaging and thoughtful in their customer service, insightful and innovative in their shop design who went bust or gave up because they "don't do maths" or "leave the figures to the accountant".

Harsh truth #2 Your accountant won't prevent you from losing money, they'll just charge you for telling you that your business has gone bust!

I'll bet some of you are sitting there at this very moment, justifying to yourselves why this chapter doesn't apply to you! So before you skip the page, glance over my myths about business plans.

#1 Planning takes away flexibility. Well no, actually planning gives you flexibility as the very best plans are constantly being reviewed and updated to reflect reality

#2 I don't need one – it's all in my head. It might well be that you have a perfectly formed vision of your business in all it's glory in your head - but it's just that, a vision. Life happens. I promise you that the reality won't look like your vision, so get real, write down the vision and be prepared to adjust to realise your dream.

#3 It's all about the ideas. Ideas are two a penny. Do you think Howard Schultz (CEO of Starbucks) was the first person to come up with the idea of a coffee shop? It's all in the execution of the idea. And that takes planning!

#4 It's only any good for getting funding. In truth your business plan is of more value to you than to any investor or bank, and investors might say that they never read business plans - what they don't tell you is that they have staff who do that for them!

The Business of Chocolate.

The purpose of a business is twofold...1) to provide you with a living or lifestyle by 2) offering a service or product for which people are prepared to pay. That's it. So far, so simple. And yet, that second part is often woefully overlooked. In our enthusiasm and passion to produce the embodiment of our vision, we entrepreneurs are all too often guilty of forgetting that our vision must also serve, or solve a problem for, a customer base, otherwise we have no business.

What "problems" might a chocolate shop solve?...It's a family member's birthday, the customer needs a gift which says " I chose these especially for you", the customer is out and about shopping a needs a cup of coffee or a chocolate fix, the customer has relatives visiting and they want somewhere exciting to take them. These are the "problems" you solve.

Encouraging customers to come to you rather than the competition is the finer detail of the problem solving, but never forget the purpose of your business – serve the customer, not your own ego!

Self Indulgence

People love to treat themselves to a chocolate Treat. If your shop looks inviting and you're in a touristic area then you are part of that touristic experience where people will treat themselves to chocolates to eat whilst meandering.

This is one of the nicest aspects of running a chocolate shop as your customers are almost always relaxed and happy.

All of our own chocolate shops have been in touristic areas with lots of weekend visitors from London. Consequently we offered a level of sophistication equal to the finest London stores. You'll need to judge your own location and customer base and we'll talk about that in detail as location is a make or break choice.

3: *We sold for several years through Liberty London. Their chocolate room has a high touristic footfall.*

Gifting

At particular times of the year people have a need for a gift – Christmas is the number one in the UK followed by Easter, then we have birthdays, thank you occasions, Mother's Day, Father's Day, Valentine's, exam results, teachers gifts etc.

So you are solving the problem of a gift, chocolates make a great gift and can be given again and again.

So the question then becomes what is unique about your chocolate shop that would make people want to choose you over say a supermarket or other chocolate brand. That's a little harder to answer but as a specialist shop you will be able to curate your collection, advise the customer, and perhaps with a fresh chocolate counter allow the customer to make their own choices offering a unique gift.

As a chocolate shop you will be heavily weighted to Christmas and Easter purchases. We'll talk about seasonality later but unless you're a very small shop you'll almost certainly need to find ways to even out some of the seasonal fluctuations.

Seasonality

You probably already have an inkling that chocolate purchases are seasonal, but you probably don't realise just how seasonal.

In the UK Christmas is the number one selling season for chocolate with a long run in of around six weeks retail. Most chocolate shops will want their Christmas range in place after the October half term holiday. It peaks the weekend before Christmas depending which day Christmas Day falls.

Easter is the number two chocolate selling season with a run in of around two weeks peaking on Easter Saturday. It is complicated as Easter moves by up to a month producing a compressed selling peak when Easter falls in March. Easter Saturday was always our busiest day of the year.

As a chocolate shop you absolutely have to hit these two selling seasons to compensate for the quieter times. It's all about the averages and for some parts of the year you'll be breaking even at best.

So what can you do increase sales in the quieter times?

For a successful shop you'll need to create some retail theatre. So you'll want to cycle your window displays and range to hit the current on trend occasion.

The graph below shows actual shop sales for a small chocolate shop and cafe for the years 2012 and 2013. Easter sales in particular vary as Easter changes each year. They are compressed with an earlier Easter and more spread out with a later Easter, but the average over the period is similar.

Shop Sales Example

The Chocolate calendar.

January – January is the worst month for all retailers and particularly chocolate retailers. Everyone is on a diet, people are broke from Christmas, and pay day is a long way away as most people were paid early before Christmas. Short of shutting down for the month – this is a good time to take a holiday or redecorate the shop. You could consider a health food push such as the current Raw Chocolate trend, but generally January is a write off for everyone except Gymnasiums. You could run a January sale but be aware if you mark down too many times it's harder to carry a higher price.

The preceding period between Christmas and New Year is quite busy and people often buy chocolates to take to New Years Eve parties. So though you'll be exhausted from Christmas you should open for a few days in this holiday period. January 1st is when the tumble weed starts!

Valentine's Day

Once you open a chocolate shop you'll realise why Valentine's Day was created. It's the first chance to kick start the retail business post Christmas. It's not a prolonged selling occasion and tends to be a two day peak characterised by lots of last minute purchases by men who've never walked into a chocolate shop before!

Whilst hearts are the popular choice it makes sense to buy stock wisely and either customise standard products with added ribbons and gift wrap or buy products that will carry over to Mother's Day.

4: A Valentines window display helps to kick start sales after the January doldrums

If you have a pick your own chocolate counter prepare some pre-made boxes for those last minute desperation purchases!

Mothers Day

In the UK the timing of Mother's Day varies depending on the Easter date. It starts the pickup of sales in the run-up to Easter. Again you can go a long way by customising standard products with ribbons and gift tags to avoid special stock purchases. They can then be tweaked as Spring or Easter collections if they don't sell.

Easter

This is the second biggest chocolate selling season in the UK. Sales build for around two weeks peaking on Easter Saturday. If the weather is good - not raining and not too hot, Easter Saturday will most likely be the busiest day of the year. To put it in context we would typically take as much on Easter Saturday as the first three weeks of January combined!

Easter eggs are the biggest seller and though there is competition this will be one of the two times of the year when people will seek you out. You really need to hit Easter with everything you can to make the most of this huge sales period. The money you make here will carry you through May and June which are often surprisingly quiet. Typically sales do not really hit a high again until the end of school term and start of the holidays in July.

It's a mistake not to stock Easter eggs as everyone expects a specialist chocolate shop to carry Easter eggs. But getting the numbers correct can be a challenge and you'll need to work closely with your supplier to avoid too much excess stock after Easter.

5: Easter is a good time to open a pop up shop

May and June Bank Holidays

Whilst holidays always help sales, particularly with shoppers and day trippers May and June can be quiet months.

Depending on your customer demographic you may wish to cater for other religious festivals. The festival of Eid for example.

Thank you Teachers and holidays

The mid to end of July sales lift with Teachers thank you gifts. A growing phenomenon small chocolate gifts and lollies make the perfect token. Again consider printed tags to customise year round stock.

The start of the School holidays is busy if you're in a touristic region and you'll also be busy with thank you gifts when people have stayed with relatives. Our own shop was in a touristic area and we used to find the start of the holidays in particular was very busy.

October Half Term

Once school holidays are over it's a quieter time again until the October school half term.

Halloween

Halloween is a huge industry in the US and is rapidly growing in the UK. Our own experience is that people are generally looking for low cost items and attempts to take it higher end have been largely unsuccessful. Nonetheless a potential for a novelty window display and the chance to boost sales.

November 5th

Though a fun occasion not necessarily a chocolate one. Our own attempts to specifically target bonfire night had limited success. But in theory it should be a good opportunity to sell hot chocolate.

Christmas

This is the big one. Everyone buys chocolates for somebody at Christmas and this is your chance to earn enough money to carry you into the next year. With cash flow projections you'll have a very good idea immediately after Christmas if you've made enough to carry you through January and stock purchases for Easter.

I recall speaking to at least two different business owners in the process of opening their first shops who said that they'd do a soft opening after Christmas. Don't do this! If you stand any chance of opening before Christmas grab the opportunity. Use a cash box if you don't have a till, buy an izettle or Paypal card reader if you don't have a card terminal – just open and sell!

We've looked at short term property leases where the landlord wanted us to continue through January to pick up Valentine's Day business. We didn't and neither should you.

I once spoke to a lovely lady at a Christmas food fair telling me she was opening a pop up shop in January and the landlord was really keen and helpful. Of course they were! Don't do this! Open before Christmas or wait until February at the earliest.

6: We became renowned for our window displays

Christmas is a fabulous opportunity to make a glorious window display. Make sure you are well stocked and aware of your supplier order cut-off dates.

24

What to sell?

Before you can design your shop layout you'll need to decide what are the main products in your product mix, and importantly -*What will my unique selling point be?*

So what will make your offering different from the supermarket? If you buy purely cash and carry items it is likely you will overlap with the supermarket offerings but are unlikely to compete on price. So as a small business you will need to work harder to find a unique product offering.

Several potential routes that might identify you as a unique specialist are...

- Pick your own fresh chocolate counter

- Chocolate gifting

- Specialist small batch bean to bar chocolate

- Raw Chocolate

- Patisserie

- Ice Cream

- Hot Chocolate, Coffee, Tea

The unique offering in our own shop was our sumptuous fresh chocolate counter.

Lets consider these in more detail.

A FRESH CHOCOLATE COUNTER

A pick your own chocolate counter allows you to offer your customers a unique selling point - the ability to create a unique selection of chocolates chosen by them. To present a gift that they have put some thought into. It also allows passing tourists or meandering shoppers the chance to visit your shop and choose a few chocolate to wander and enjoy.

Illustration

7: This fresh chocolate counter utilise two layers of each chocolate with clear perspex to keep the display looking full whilst rotating stock

You will of course need to choose a fresh chocolate supplier or several suppliers. Here is another area where you can go for a more mass produced imported Belgian chocolate or an artisan handmade chocolate from a company such ourselves - Lick the Spoon.

Surprisingly before we opened our fresh chocolate counter we had no idea if it would work, particularly as many of the chocolates had a short shelf life of 6 weeks meaning a relative fast turnaround was required. Fortunately we needn't have worried as it proved to be the most successful aspect of our shop.

A pick your own chocolate counter will in theory also allow you to achieve greater profit margins. The reason being that the chocolates are supplied to you loose for you to package. When a manufacturer pre-packages chocolates he has to charge you for staff to pack them. With a pick your own counter you can either pre-package some boxes in quieter moments or allow your customers to self serve making more efficient use of your time and building the staff costs to package into your own staff costs retaining more of the profit in your business!

But there are many small Delis and chocolate shops that try to implement similar counters and get it completely wrong. We'll explain how we set up our chocolate counter with our top tips and benefit of experience in the appendix of this book.

As a specialist chocolate shop a pick your own counter adds a unique customer experience usually only replicated in the largest of luxury store food halls.

Chocolate Gifting Occasions

We've already described the chocolate calendar and you will want to cycle your product range to hit all of those gifting occasions - Easter Eggs at Easter, Thank you teacher gifts etc.

There will be a number of longer shelf life chocolate products that will be suitable for gifting all year round. You'll need these longer shelf life items to complement your shorter shelf life fresh chocolates.

Favourites include Chocolate Coated Ginger, Chocolate dipped Orange, Honeycomb, Chocolate Bars and Drops, Hot Chocolate, themed Chocolate Lollies.

All of these items allow you target the specific gifting occasions that your customers will seek you out for.

SPECIALIST BEAN TO BAR CHOCOLATE

In the last five years the newest trend in artisan chocolate has been the so called 'bean to bar' or Craft chocolate movement. Bean to Bar is the tag line that has been adopted by small scale chocolate makers who either source cocoa beans direct from the growers, or simply buy ready roasted cocoa nibs and grind them with sugar (and milk powder for milk chocolate) before tempering them into chocolate bars. The movement is similar to the craft beer or coffee movement.

More recently the term 'Tree to bar' has become popular as cocoa growers are starting to produce their own chocolate on the plantation.

An example of Tree to Bar is the wonderful Crayfish Bay plantation in Grenada where owners Kim and Lylette roast their own beans on a home made charcoal roaster. We were fortunate enough to stay on their plantation and help advise them on the set up of their tempering room.

Offering a range of specialist bean to bar chocolate allows you to tell the story of and connect with the chocolate makers and cocoa growers that is difficult for a Supermarket to do.

You may even wish to consider buying a small grinder* such as those supplied by www.bean-to-bar.co.uk and grinding some cocoa nibs in store. This will add retail theatre and create a wonderful aroma as well as the chance for chocolate making workshops.

They are quite noisy however and you should check your insurance in terms of unattended machinery.

8: The availabilty of low cost small scale grinders has contributed to the increase in the number of bean-to-bar chocolate makers

If you're opening in a trendy urban area such as Brick Lane in London or feel like taming your hipster beard this could be the market for you!

RAW CHOCOLATE

An even more recent trend is the Raw Food movement and within that Raw Chocolate. The premise here is that Raw, that is uncooked food, is healthier for you. With Raw chocolate the bean roasting stage is omitted and sugar substitutes that are 'considered' healthier are often used to further bolster health claims.

There is some controversy surrounding the Raw chocolate makers. Some non Raw chocolate makers argue vehemently that the temperatures reached during fermentation and grinding exceed the Raw Food movements temperature guidelines for Raw food. We've seen some Raw chocolate marketed as 'cold pressed' which is an interesting concept given the fat part of the bean - cocoa butter - is solid at room temperature!

Our opinion on Raw chocolate is taste it, if you like it or more importantly think your customers will like it then consider it.

It is starting to appear in supermarkets but as many producers are still small scale it could be a chance to experiment stocking an early trend.

We explore Raw chocolate in greater detail in the appendix of this book.

PATISSERIE

One of the elements we always felt that was the missing piece in our Chocolate shop was a Patisserie counter. Whilst as a manufacturer we made beautiful bespoke wedding cakes, brownies and other small cakes, we didn't specialise in French style patisserie for our shop. It wasn't for lack of capability so much as simply too many different products in a small manufacturing space. We intuitively felt that there was a missing space in the British high street for this as most bakeries offered low price sticky iced buns. In most other European countries every small town has a wonderful Patisserie and bakery of a quality rarely seen in the UK.

The big problem with Patisserie or indeed any fresh food, sandwiches etc., is wastage. As a shop if you aren't turning over cakes daily you'll need to throw them or give them away.

The way this is managed by stores such as Patisserie Valerie is to store as frozen and then put out to defrost in a chilled display cabinet. This way if you're careful you can reduce your deliveries and adjust your display to suit footfall patterns, more at weekends etc.

Unfortunately there are almost no high quality wholesale Patisserie suppliers in the UK and this is the main reason we didn't introduce such a counter. We'll explore Patisserie options furthe in the appendix of this book.

9: A cake display in our window proved popular but wasn't the full patisserie offering we would have liked

After we sold our shop business we did identify such a supplier named Patisserie Box in Cheltenham who now have a Patisserie counter next to our chocolate counter in a busy farm shop! Classic Fine Foods also sell a range of potentially interesting products such as frozen macaroons. If you have an Ice cream display freezer for example it's possible to store sealed Macaroons in the storage compartment. Even without a refrigerated display they can be taken out daily as they defrost within minutes to give a beautiful Macaroon display.

Patisserie could be the perfect complement to your chocolate range.

ICE CREAM

As soon as the outside temperature rises to 25 degrees C or the day is sunny chocolate sales will naturally fall. If you're unlucky this can even happen at Easter. We experienced an Easter that was so hot that customers didn't want to buy Easter eggs for fear they might melt on the way to the car - disaster! But more generally than this people simply don't want to eat chocolate on a hot sunny day.

The natural counterpoint to this is Ice Cream.

If you retail Ice cream incredibly well of course then there would be no need to sell chocolates. There is an Italian Gelato we know in Bath that sells Ice cream all year round even on the coldest days, and they are always busy. Part of the reason is they are the only people in town making really smooth Italian Gelato, their display cabinet looks lovely and enticing, and they are on the tourist route. They also have a great reputation and we always visit them ourselves.

So, if you have the space and can partner with a really fine Gelato supplier you could be onto a winner. There is a down side however - beautiful sloped and curved Italian style display freezers are really expensive, in the order of several thousand pounds, potentially at least £10,000. Second hand freezers can also be a risky purchase and you'll need to factor in the potential need for repairs. Refrigerated items are the one area where it's worth buying new if you can afford to.

For our own shop we opened without an Ice cream cabinet and then rapidly began to explore Ice Cream as the first spell of warm weather approached in our first year. We were unable to find a suitable Italian style Gelato supplier so opted for the best regional Ice cream maker we could find. Similarly we couldn't afford a large Gelato cabinet so we opted for the best affordable glass fronted Ice cream freezer we could - flat glass and recessed Ice cream Bain Marie's that are a little harder to see from a distance. It was a white plastic freezer so we bought a roll of wood veneer and cut and stuck it around the freezer front and sides. This was actually surprisingly effective and fitted with the visual style of our shop.

10: Moving the Ice Cream outside on a busy day increased sales

As the freezer was a later addition we made a layout error as in order to access the freezer the member of staff serving needed to leave the till and run around the shop counter to serve at the freezer. On busy days we kept a small second till by the freezer or used a money belt and would dial in the Ice cream sales later.

On sunny summer weekends we would wheel the freezer outside the front of the shop and would station someone serving there under a big umbrellas. This worked very well as it attracted people looking down the street who might have missed us, added a bit of retail theatre, and removed the mental barrier that customers have of making the effort to walk into a shop on a hot day.

11: Sunny days are great for outside sales

Ice cream is the perfect complement to chocolate in the summer and a scooping cabinet offers a unique selling point over supermarkets and convenience stores.

HOT CHOCOLATE

If you're considering an ancillary café as part of your chocolate shop then specialising in Hot Chocolate can be a great speciality addition and the obvious choice for a chocolate shop.

As a speciality shop I would recommend going beyond the ubiquitous packet mixes to making your own hot chocolate using real chocolate. There are several ways you could do this...

Hot Chocolate Lickable Spoons - ok a blatant plug here, but our Hot Chocolate Lickable Spoons ® are one solution. Use your coffee machine to steam milk and present the cup of steaming milk with a hot chocolate Lickable spoon. The customer then stirs in the spoon to create a delicious hot chocolate. The stirring of the spoon is part of the experience.

Check out our You Tube channel @lickthespoonUK for a demonstration of making a hot chocolate with a Lickable Spoon. We also have some footage filmed in Madagscar with Chocolat Madagscar making a Madagascan hot chocolate.

Flaked hot chocolate – some chocolatiers use a machine to create a flaked hot chocolate from real chocolate. This can also be mixed with steamed milk to create a hot chocolate.

Italian style chocolate machine – these have a Bain-marie at the base to heat the hot chocolate and keep it warm and a paddle to rotate the hot chocolate and keep it incorporated and even in temperature. We used one of these machines in our shop and also occasionally at food festivals. They work well.

We made up our own hot chocolate recipe each morning using small drops of chocolate and fresh milk. We would heat the milk in a jug using the steam wand of our coffee machine until steaming. We would then whisk in the drops of chocolate whilst continuing to steam and whisk. The drops would not only melt into the milk, but by simmering and whisking would be emulsified in. Effectively forming a very milky ganache. Once fully whisked in we would pour it into the hot chocolate machine which would then keep it available for continuous use throughout the day.

- Advantages – hot chocolate continuously on tap for fast service during busy periods. Can also be used as a hot sauce for Ice Cream sundaes.

- Disadvantage – if you make too much you may need throw it away at the end of the day.

12: *We used a hot chocolate machine at markets even before we opened a shop*

As the hot chocolate effectively forms a hot hold ganache we would reuse a fresh batch a maximum of two times by running off any unused hot chocolate each night into a jug, allowing to cool, then refrigerating over night. The next morning we would use the steam wand and whisk to reheat the hot chocolate. A paper record was kept each day so a maximum of two refrigerations were noted before throwing away. In busy times we would use all of the hot chocolate in a day or sometimes two batches.

As a chocolate shop offering specialist hot chocolate is a natural choice that many customers will expect.

TIP: Use your hot chocolate as a hot Ice Cream sauce or to make a mocha coffee.

COFFEE & TEA

The high street is abound with coffee shops so you'll need to be at the top of your game to compete as a pure coffee shop. We partnered with Brian Wogan coffee roasters in Bristol for our coffee. We chose a Java bean with our own roast chosen to complement chocolate but also drink well on its own. Our own shop was small so we chose a smaller two group coffee machine and ran it by Brian Wogan before purchase. If you're buying second hand as mentioned earlier make sure your machine is serviced before use and is noted on your insurance. As a pressurised vessel they can be dangerous.

Our machine was set up by Wogan coffee and we also received some barista training from them. We chose a smaller menu than many coffee shops as our aim was to be a speciality chocolate shop and we couldn't offer every variation of coffee. For a mocha we made use of our excellent hot chocolate and for cappuccino we topped with cocoa powder in the Italian way.

We had a small electric grinder next to our machine and we used this to grind beans almost to order to keep them as flavoursome as possible.

Coffee machines are relatively easy to run and produce excellent coffee when set up and maintained correctly. They need to be cleaned each night and this takes around 10 minutes. The margins in coffee are generally very good if you consider the cost of beans relative to the cost of a cup of coffee. As with fresh chocolates, scooping Ice Cream and serving hot chocolate, you are providing the labour.

Tea – we partnered with Sherston Teas for our tea offering and chose a small range of high quality teas and infusions. Again opting for quality over quantity. Hot water was provided by our coffee machine and we used loose leaf tea in elegant but modern individual pots that sat on top of the cups.

We viewed tea, coffee and hot chocolate sales as a way of cross selling and up selling our chocolates and supplementing overall sales. So we offered a chocolate as a 'bit on the side' with a drink at 60p extra (at the time). Cake and coffee combination buys also worked well – coffee and a cake for £4 for example. With hindsight a larger shop would have allowed us to make more of our coffee and cake offering. We had three internal tables with a total of 10 seats. We supplemented this with 5 fold-up outdoor tables and chairs with brightly coloured table cloths that worked well in the good weather or for dog owners (we didn't allow dogs in the shop with the exception of guide dogs). Even on miserable days the bright table cloths acted as a visual sign that our shop was open.

PROS:

- A small specialist offering of tea and coffee allows the opportunity to cross sell chocolates and give customers another reason to enter your shop.

- Margins on Tea & Coffee are good as you are providing the labour.

CONS:

- You will need more staff on busy days to clear tables and additional equipment for dishwashing.

- Competition is high so you will need to be at the top of your game.

Illustration

13: Even on miserable days outside seating indicated we were open

We've presented several options to consider in your product mix. You'll see more details on the set up requirements for these later in this book and also how to add them into your sales projections in our business plan in the appendix.

Options such as a coffee machine and Ice Cream freezer could significantly affect your shop layout and back of house requirements so you need to plan these into your shop layout.

So onwards to the next section – how to choose your shop location!

Opening a Shop

Location, location, location

It may be a cliché but Phil and Kirsty had it right - the location of your shop will make or break your business. One of the first shocks you encounter when considering opening a shop is just how high retail rents are in the UK and indeed many other countries world wide. It can be easy to mistake an annual rent for the purchase price in some prime locations! This can lead you to look at all sorts of properties in back street locations which the agent will sell you as up and coming or offering great potential.

The specific challenge with a chocolate shop is that you're selling chocolate!...if you're selling diamonds, you only might need one sale a day to cover your overheads. The lower the price point of your goods, the more sales you need to put through. It doesn't mean it can't work - if you stand and count the number of sales going through the Poundland tills, you'll quickly see that the money is flowing in despite the low price tag.

When we were first looking for a shop location, our children were small. Like many small businesses that started from home, we had a vision of a combined shop and production facility close to where we lived.

Two chocolate shops have since opened and closed in our town. One was a small independent shop. They opened in a location at the top of town at the point just past where people stopped and turned back.

The second shop was a larger combined card and chocolate shop in a prime rental location. It sold cheaper mass produced brands of chocolates but still failed. Location is everything!

We live very close to the touristic city of Bath and this seemed like an ideal location for a chocolate shop. However a closer look at the city showed that tourists tended to follow a particular route around the famous sites. The rental in these locations was enormous! We have run pop up shops three times in Bath. The first was run for 10 days in the run up to Easter opposite Jamie Oliver's restaurant. Though we only leased this for ten days we spent £60 on window graphics giving the air of a more permanent shop at relatively low cost. This was very successful and was a location we would have liked to try longer but the long term lease was given to Jamie to open a deli.

14: Our first Easter pop up shop opposite Jamie Oliver's restaurant was a big success

The second pop up shop in Bath was in almost the same location but down a stair way. This wasn't successful and demonstrated to us just how important location is.

Our third pop-up shop was more successful. Situated next to a busy cafe and opposite Carluccio's restaurant we ran outside tastings to encourage people inside. But it still wasn't as successful as the first location opposite Jamie Oliver's restaurant.

Illustration 15: Our third pop-up shop. Outside tasters encouraging customers inside

We opened our permanent shop in the historic town of Cirencester. I was delivering Easter Eggs to a new stockists opened there and was blown away by the fantastic chic yet sympathetic redevelopment of the old corn hall in the centre of town. I was so excited I immediately telephoned Diana telling her I had found the shop location! It seemed perfect - a historic town, a beautiful redevelopment, weekend London clientele, a chic new restaurant and relatively low rentals compared with Bath. We immediately asked to view the vacant unit and were particularly keen on the unit opposite the restaurant.

Unfortunately the landlord didn't want to place us opposite the restaurant in case of competition so we were shown a corner unit in their other new development in town. It was yet to be completed so we couldn't assess footfall, but the shop was in beautiful Cotswold stone with a double window out of direct sunshine. The unit was shown as the new foodie quarter on the council redevelopment plan and the road was to be pedestrianised. Other units had been signed up by interesting independent retailers and it seemed to be a potentially great location at a relatively affordable rental of £12,000 per year. I say relatively, we had looked at some units in central bath with an annual rental of 10 times that amount! We also instinctively felt that a corner location like this would always be leasable in the future. We signed up!

16: *Our Cirencester Shop was a shell when we first viewed it but the location felt good*

With the benefit of hindsight (which is what you're paying for in the purchase of this book!) we would have been more analytical in our evaluation of premises.

My thoughts on the subject 10 years on...

Combined retail and production space, advantages;

- only one rent and rates bill to pay
- eligible for small business rates relief if you have only one location (current policy as of 2017)
- less staffing required
- efficient use of quiet times in the shop

disadvantages;

- price per square meter is much higher for retail space, so you are effectively paying over the odds for your production space.
- Planning permissions for change of use may be needed and not necessarily granted
- access for deliveries may be restricted in high footfall areas

Opening in your home town

- Should only be considered if the location, footfall and demographic of the people fit the needs of your business.

Golden rules of location

- Make sure you are in an area where people will walk by. This includes making sure you are the right side of the street – some busy looking streets have one side which is much busier than the other. If you are the other side, is it easy for people to cross? If it is busy, is it only people rushing to and from work? Are they likely to stop and browse? Are they there at the weekends too? If they all work in offices or banks, is the street busy with shoppers the rest of the time?

- You get what you pay for – cheap rent probably means low footfall, so stand outside the premises on different days at different times and literally count the number of passers by

- Look for other luxury retailers – if you are surrounded only by pound shops and discount retailers, chances are it's the wrong spot for high end purchases

- if you're selling chocolates, check the aspect – avoid any south facing windows!

Estimating Footfall in a location

One of the most difficult things when choosing a location is assessing just how busy you will be. For whilst you can build footfall through reputation and advertising you'll have a pretty good idea within a month of opening as to whether you're likely to be a success. By which time it may be too late! You'll need to assess potential sales for your business plan and we'll show a simple spreadsheet to do this later. The downside of spreadsheets is it's really easy to tweak the numbers to persuade yourself that you'll soon be sailing off to the Caribbean on your profits! Almost everyone instinctively overestimates their sales at first.

One technique we used to 'guesstimate' our sales was to camp outside a well known chocolate shop surreptitiously counting customers. But to gain an accurate picture you'll need to do this over all days of the week and at different seasons. You can refer to our graph showing sales variations across the year to give yourself an idea as to how this might vary seasonally.

TIP Scout out a similar business in a similar location to see just how busy they are to give an idea of your own footfall.

Estimating profitability of similar businesses in a location

Another technique you can use to assess the viability of a location is to discretely look at the accounts of similar businesses in that location or similar locations. Companies house in the UK has a free online service that lets you view the accounts of all limited companies. Not all businesses will be limited companies but some in your chosen location will.

At the time of writing the url is https://beta.companieshouse.gov.uk

Companies house will only show abbreviated Balance Sheet accounts, but with a bit of detective work you can work out how much profit a business has made. Look at the Profit and Loss line and calculate the change between the previous year and the current year. This change will be the operating profit after depreciation. If the numbers are shown in brackets they are negative representing a loss, but the change can still be positive indicating a profit. The brackets are not necessarily a bad thing as many businesses put in start up loans, so long as the change is moving in the right direction. But the size of the number in the brackets should be proportional to a start up loan that the business owners might have put in. If it's too large a negative figure proportional to the shop size then alarm bells should ring. There are other free websites that will show the accounts over several years and you might want to view these to see continued profit.

For example ....

2016   2015

Profit and loss account(40,000)   (60,000)

Indicating an operating profit of 20,000 in the year 2015 to 2016 after depreciation. This company's accumulated balance sheet loss has been reduced from 60k to 40k. Depreciation is an amount offset over time against profit for equipment or assets purchased. So if the business has invested in the purchase of new equipment depreciation can be relatively high.

Most small businesses that set up as a limited company will pay their owner directors a tax efficient relatively low wage and take the rest as profit dividends or start up director's loan repayments. So you can 'guesstimate' what the owners might be earning based on the profit and loss and an assumed low tax threshold wage.

For example the low tax rate threshold might be 9k per year so you could assume that the company directors are both earning 9k plus the potential to withdraw some of the profit as dividends or loan repayments.

The most important thing that can be gleaned from the accounts is that apparently successful businesses may not be profitable ones. This could stop you building your business location and strategy on a house of cards! You will of course be friends and neighbours with many of these businesses so be discrete! This free service didn't exist when we opened our first shop but it could have really helped our location assessments.

TIP Discretely check the abbreviated balance sheets of similar businesses for free online at Companies House to see if they are profitable in your chosen location.

The Indiana Jones Effect

Remember the ray of light shine through the glass in the Indiana Jones film burning a hole? Well that's what will happen to your chocolate window display if you have a south facing window. Even on a cool winter's day a ray of sun can melt chocolate through a window. So whilst not so ideal for most shops, choose your chocolate shop location carefully such that your window won't be in direct sun light. You may have seen chocolate shops in this situation that have resorted to cardboard window displays.

Check the orientation on a map before you even go to look at a shop!

17: Avoid the sunny side of the street with a chocolate shop!

To Buy or to Lease?

I imagine for almost everyone reading this the only option in the modern era is to lease a premises. Sadly property prices have risen to such an extent that even the annual rental in a good location can be mistaken for a purchase price when you first start looking at retail property! However if you do have money to invest in property do consider the location and likely return on your investment carefully. Will it leave you enough cash to survive the early months of business? If you don't have enough cash your business may fail before you become profitable!

As an investment property has historically increased in value over time, plus you won't need to pay rent to a landlord. However it may make you less focussed on making the business a success. Think of those sad small shops you may have seen that look like the owners gave up decades ago, but somehow continue to trade as the business owner also owns the premises.

If you don't have enough up front cash to purchase a premises but have accumulated pensions in previous jobs an option that is available in the UK at the time of writing is the Self Invested Personal Pension or SIPP. SIPPs allow you to transfer money in from existing personal pensions and use the pension pot to purchase commercial property. The business then pays rent at the going rate to the SIPP. Thus your business is funding your pension! You should take independent financial advice before ploughing all of your pension into the purchase of a retail premises and don't let your eagerness cloud your judgement on location!

We ourselves used the SIPP option to purchase our production premises, but not our retail shops which have always been leased, here are a few of the Pros and Cons we found...

SIPP Pros

- Your business rent funds your pension rather than an anonymous landlord.

- Your SIPP can be used to pay for building maintenance

- You can give yourself favourable lease terms, though they would still need to be considered commercial. So rental levels will be at commercial rent values but you can write in the ability to terminate the lease at any time.

- Historically property has been a good investment increasing in value

- You won't be at the whims of your landlord, though you will have to keep your SIPP informed of insurance and rental details

SIPP Cons

- Expect high legal fees and complexity to set up.

- All your pension eggs are in one basket

- You still need to pay a solicitor to draw up a lease

- You need to periodically pay for independent chartered surveyors to set rental at the current going rate. Perhaps surprisingly you have no direct control over rental levels as SIPPS are governed by HMRC rules.

- When you want to retire you will need to sell the premises

TO LEASE

For most people leasing is the most likely way to secure a retail premises. Fortunately in recent years some landlords have implemented more flexible leases though it's still one of the most critical decisions you're likely to make.

Historically most leases were based on a fixed term say 5 years or 10 years. The landlord would typically be a property developer and the retail unit would be placed in a management company. The lease forms a legal agreement with the management company and might cover areas such as...

- Annual Rental - traditionally billed quarterly in advance

- Annual Service charge - covering emptying of common bins, maintenance of common areas, employment of a caretaker etc.

- Defines which areas of the property you will maintain and insure and which the landlord will maintain and insure

- Other responsibilities, opening hours, types of business permitted etc.

Essentially you will need to employ a solicitor to look over and help negotiate the wording of the legal aspects of your lease.

If this seems a bit daunting, well, it is! Fortunately with the economic turmoil since 2009 and the decline of the high street in the UK, some flexibility has appeared in recent years.

TURNOVER BASED LEASES

A number of landlords have introduced more flexible turnover based leases. We ran a pop-up shop in a shopping centre in historic Bath for three months on this basis.

Unless you have a proven model and are absolutely certain of your turnover this would seem to be a perfect solution. The landlord will typically set a minimal rental plus a weekly or monthly rental based on a negotiated percentage of your turnover, 10% say. So if you have a quiet month, as January often is, your turnover is low. A busy month and your rental is higher, but in proportion.

Are there any disadvantages?

Well you will have to report your turnover to your landlord. Consequently you'll have much closer contact with them or their management team and they are likely to keep a very close eye on you. It came to light in the Bath shopping centre we rented that management were monitoring customers in and out of our shop with CCTV. So big brother will be watching you!

With a fixed rental your landlord will most likely leave you alone on a day to day basis. In our Cirencester shop we lived in peaceful coexistence with our landlord, but the rental was the same no matter how quiet the shop was.

Nonetheless if I were opening a new retail business today a turnover based rental would have great appeal and would probably be our preference. A word of caution though. The more flexible landlords have often had to be as their retail units aren't as busy as they could be.

TIP Check the turnover the rent is based on is net of VAT. Even if you aren't initially VAT registered. You don't want to be paying rental on your VAT!

LEASE NEGOTIATION TIPS

Negotiating a lease is a tricky thing and you will probably want to seek all of the help you can get. Here are some of our experiences.

If you are going into a new shopping centre the centre management team will always want to attract the big name anchor stores, and as an unknown independent it will be difficult to obtain a good bargaining position or first bite at the best positions. An example of this we encountered was the relatively new South-gate shopping centre in Bath. All of the prime spots were reserved by big brand names months in advance. By the time we came to look only a few retail units were left in slightly odd positions. There was however the Little South gate corridor designed for independents. Though one look at this corridor and you could see it was a dead zone. There are now some excellent stores there, but I'm sure they would agree that the turnover of independent shops in that corridor has been far too high since opening.

The sales team of the centre were also a little hazy shall we say during negotiations, stating that a major national Chocolate retailer had no interest in the centre at all and had ruled it out of their plans. You guessed it, a couple of months later the same retailer opened there in a prime spot that must have been agreed long before we had started to look. Fortunately we had enough experience to walk away and decided that it wasn't right for us. The shopping centre was more suited to the national retailer.

What length of lease?

This is a tricky one. It will be swayed by how much money you are sending to fit out the shop and how good the position is. If you go for a 5 year lease and spend a significant amount of money fitting out the shop there is no guarantee that the landlord will renew the lease at the end of the period. Though in practice if you are a good tenant and pay your rent on time there's no reason they shouldn't.

But if you opt for a 10 year lease and realise after a year that the location just doesn't work for you what will you do?

The solution to this is to get an assignable lease with a number of potential lease break periods.

Assignable Lease

An assignable lease allows you to sell the remainder of your lease to another business. So if circumstances change or you need to change the location or the structure of your business you have a means to do this. We ourself used this method when we sold our retail shop business allowing us to transfer the lease to a new company.

The landlord will have had a solicitor write the lease so there are usually clauses governing the assignment and it may even return to you should the assignee stop paying rent! But is a valuable asset and you should aim for an assignable lease. After some discussion our landlord allowed a new lease to be created for the new owner rather than assigning our lease when we sold our shop, and this removed any possibility of the shop returning to us in bad circumstances, and allowed the new owners a lease of their own.

Lease Breaks

A lease break allows you to give notice to your landlord that you wish to stop the lease at key fixed dates, typically three years and five years. Ideally I would aim for a lease break at one year - if you've got it completely wrong you may be able to get out without going bankrupt! It should be emphasised that the lease break clause should be on your side of the agreement only! An assignable lease can help mitigate the lack of lease breaks but does require you to actively sell the lease. If your shop isn't doing so well it's going to be harder to sell the business and lease as a going concern as the interested party might simply wait until you close. Hence the advantage of lease break clauses if you decide things aren't working out.

Rent free period and Stepped Rental

Some landlords offer a rent free period for shop fitting, typically three months. It's also possible they may be open to a stepped rental. For example you pay 10k PA year 1, 11k PA year 2 etc.

The important thing with the stepped rental is to look at the end point rental – is it sustainable? Don't be lured into the initial low rental without planning for the full thing. Whilst you will build trade it's unlikely to follow the simple linear step and will follow the whims of the economic climate, your nearby competition, the weather, or the unexpected such as the council digging up the road for three months!

Illustration

18: Three months of unexpected gas works outside of our shop affected trade badly

We adopted a stepped rental on our shop just as the economic crash occurred. It became clear after a year that the steps in rental were no longer realistic with the economic climate and other expected improvements such as road pedestrianisation that hadn't occurred. We talked to our landlord, were open about our position and they were fair and agreed to hold the rent at the year 1 value. I think they could see that we had built a beautiful shop and were gaining traction, but the economy was a struggle. Not everyone got on with our landlords in the same way but we found them to be fair and generally we had little interaction.

Rent Deposit

Depending on how new your business is and if you have a trading history your landlord may require a rent deposit. This can be quite a number of months rent and you should be prepared for this potentially unexpected cash requirement in your business plan.

So Just how are rental levels set?

Levels of rent vary hugely. We looked at premise with rentals as low as a 5000 per year to 100,000 per year in varying locations.

In theory the rental level is set by a chartered surveyor who consulted the knowledge of their secret 'little book'. This divides the retail space into areas such as prime retail at the front, secondary retail further back, and then toilet area, upper floors etc. Each area is allocated a nominal pound/sq ft or sq m value. You can get an idea of how the rental for a given shop is calculated by looking up the rateable value of a property.

In theory the rateable value of a property is the nominal annual rent that property can achieve and it is possible to see how this is calculated on the local authority website, assuming it is an existing building that has been rated.

Back of house areas and upper floors are usually calculated at a much lower pound per square foot than the prime retail area.

Location of the property also makes a difference of course and shops in a prime footfall area will attract higher rent.

The sad reality is that property in the UK is at a premium and rental levels are really much higher than any sane person would consider.

When we first looked at retail rentals in our local town shopping centre the great 2009 crash had just occurred. We assumed that as there were several empty units that it would be possible to negotiate the rental level. However it transpired that after completion in the 1980s the shopping centre had been sold by the town council to a pension fund. As a valuable asset on their balance sheet reducing rentals could eventually lead to a write down on the value of the asset. Thus it was in the pension funds interest to keep the advertised rental level even if the shop stayed empty!

The centre has struggled in subsequent years and though there have been some pop-up shop initiatives units are frequently empty.

Sadly you may find this the case when you try to negotiate. The landlord may have bank funding and will need to get their sign off on any rental negotiation. But you should try to negotiate or walk away if the level feels too uncomfortable for your financial plans.

It can be tempting at this point to look at low rental buildings in odd locations. Don't be so desperate to set up shop that you forget how important location is! Ask for the second opinion of an impartial third party.

When we were first looking we were working with a local graphic design agency for logo design. They had some experience of shop graphics and had done some beautiful design for a Smoothie shop in Swindon that closed shortly after opening because it was in the wrong location. As we chatted about a potential shop location in our home town they said to us – are you sure that's the right location and demographic for your business? This was of course polite code for 'are you mad!'. They were right and fortunately we didn't open there.

We did find help in the form of the town council. There are good people who do want to help new businesses, and though the council had no control of the shopping centre they did have a few properties to let. The man from the council in charge of these lettings offered advice and even arranged for a surveyor the council used to look over a couple of properties free of charge to advise on rental levels.

So in summary rental levels are set by various secret calculations squirrelled away in a surveyors book, in collusion with estate agents who couldn't care less if your business is a success, encouraged by local authorities desperate for cash, and backed by pension funds who can't see their balance sheets decrease in value. It's a house of cards you'll have to do your best to negotiate – good luck!

TIP Check the local authority website for the rateable value of the property to see how the shop is divided into prime retail secondary retail etc.

TIP Ask an independent person for their opinion on the location with regards to your business. Remember whilst you want a low rent, location is key to success.

What about the Rates?

As well as rent you will need to pay business rates to the local authority. For an established property you can look up the rateable value on the local authority website. The rates payable are then a multiplier of the rateable value, typically around 40% depending on current legislation. Other factors such as small business rates relief can come into play potentially further reducing the rates payable.

So what do I get for my business rates?

Pretty much nothing! It's another form of taxation but there's little correlation to services you might receive, you won't even get your bins emptied!

How often do rates change?

Every five years or so the local authority recalculates business rates. Like the rental value it takes into account a number of arbitrary factors. It can also take into account improvements you make to the property. So rather unfairly you can be taxed more for improvements you may make! Rises in the property market and increases in your rent can also affect the rateable value.

The arbitrary nature of business rates assessment has resulted in many companies that will telephone you offering to challenge rateable values on your behalf on a no win no fee basis.

We were once in conversation with a local chocolate shop owner in a historic town centre. His shop had been leased from the council for ten years and a new lease was required. The council put the annual rental up from 45k per year to 65k per year. On top of this his rates had increased to 35k per year. So before staff costs he now had to pay 100k per year! You need to sell an awful lot of chocolates to cover such costs and not surprisingly he called it a day and the shop was put up for rent.

So in summary you'll need to factor rates into your budget and be prepared for unexpected changes.

Responsibility for Repairs

The same Chocolatier mentioned above had also fallen foul of the loathsome 'Full Repairing lease'. On the ground floor of a Georgian three storey grade 1 listed building he had been required to pay for part of the roof repairs.

We would avoid full repairing leases like the plague. The arrangement where you are responsible for the internals of the building and the landlord for the exterior is much fairer. It's possible however that the landlord may still expect you to pay for part of the buildings insurance but not for repairs. A service charge may also cover common area maintenance.

A brief discussion on insurance

It's worth touching on insurance at this point... (might be time to grab a coffee!)

You will need the following insurance...

- Buildings - probably covered by your landlord but charged back to you in some way

- Contents - covers the contents of your shop including stock, fittings, money in a night safe

- Windows - though you would think it would be covered by the landlord due to the nature of retail Windows and breakages your policy will probably need to cover this

- Public liability - insurance against accidents that may occur to the general public

- Employers liability - insurance against accidents and injury to your employees

Though this might seem quite a lot, the contents, employers liability, public liability etc. are usually all covered by a single combined policy that is not usually too expensive.

Beware of the exclusions and caveats however. Pressurised items such as coffee machines need to be mentioned, ice cream freezers and fridges, all of the usual small print designed to trip you up in insurance policies. Also be careful if you plan to make anything on premises as this may not be covered by a retail policy and may need product liability and manufacturing cover. Don't you hate insurance!

Checking Legal Requirements

Before signing your lease you'll want to check the legal requirements of your premises and this will involve contacting the local council and also environmental health officer.

Premises are classified under the Town and Country planning act with classifications such A1 – shop, A3 – Restaurant Café, etc.

You can find out full details of all of the classifications on the internet but the most likely two you'll need to be concerned with are A1 and A3 or B1 usage. Most retail shops are A1 usage meaning they are intended for retail of goods.

If you are planning to be a chocolate shop with retail only this is fine. But what if you want to also serve coffee with chocolates and perhaps cakes? It is possible to do this with A1 planning running the shop as primarily retail with an ancillary café. Each local authority takes a different view on this. The rule of thumb being that the majority of your sales come from retail sales.

A3 usage gives you full restaurant and café planning permission.

B1 usage includes "light industry appropriate in a residential area" which would cover manufacturing small quantities on site which you could sell on to third party businesses.

However there are many different departments in the council and having the planning on the premises doesn't mean that you can open a café without consulting environmental health. Consulting the environmental health department can be a little daunting and they may put requirements on you that are a 'nice to have' rather than a legal requirement. Nonetheless it's better to talk to them early in the planning process as if they're not happy with what your doing they can stop you trading!

TIP Consult Environmental health early but be prepared with background research of your own and ask them to clarify what are legal requirements and 'nice to haves'

When we opened our Cirencester shop we planned a primarily retail shop with an ancillary café. The idea was we would serve coffee with a chocolate on the side to encourage people to enjoy the chocolate shop experience. We would have a very simple cake offering – brownies etc. Our shop was an empty shell and we had planned a layout with a back of house wash up area and staff toilet. We spoke with environmental health and they were keen to look at the layout before we physically erected walls.

The usage as "ancillary café" is a grey area. Environmental health didn't mind it and we're happy with our planned wash up and hand wash facility, but wanted us to make the toilet a customer toilet. Their argument was not unreasonable that customers would want to use the toilet.

The problem was the shop area was very small – 33 sq metres. If we made the toilet customer facing we needed to have a double customer door to shield them from looking directly in the toilet, and, under new planning it needed to meet accessible sizing requirements. The practical outcome of this was the toilet would take up 1/3 of our available shop space!

We managed to argue that as an ancillary café customers could use the nearby tourist information toilet and we would keep it as a much smaller staff toilet. Environmental health were reluctant on this point but as there was no clear legal requirement they stated that they might in future pass legislation requiring a customer toilet!

Our shop was also in a conservation area. We had decided to put in an air conditioning system to keep the chocolates at the correct temperature. However we weren't allowed to put the cooling unit in sight so ended up running the pipes up the stairs underneath the flats above to an outside roof space. Enter stage left the noise department who then needed to see proof that the cooling unit would not cause undue noise to future residents.

It was worse for a nearby restaurant opening at the same time. Environmental health had determined that they needed an extraction chimney to route potential cooking smells, not from them, but for potential future occupants. The routing of the chimney had to be out of sight. Enter stage left the noise department that required they install noise baffles. So they ended up with a £15,000 bill for an extraction system they didn't think they'd need!

So it's advisable to check with the local authorities before signing a lease, but be aware they can be overzealous and so be prepared to counter red tape on grey areas if they seem impractical or unreasonable.

What will Environmental Health Require?

You will need to contact your local environmental health officer (EHO) for definitive advice, but here are some of their requirements that might affect your shop layout or fitting requirements. We'll talk about other day to day running aspects later.

Making chocolates on the premises

If you are planning the whole production on site, you have multiple challenges to face, separating the delivery, production and public areas or operating safely if in the customer facing area. I would recommend a planning meeting with the EHO before you invest any money in equipment or layout!

Selling Pre-Packaged items only

If you're selling pre-packaged items only then your requirements are minimal. Your shop will need to be rodent proof and this might ring alarm bells in buildings which are old, listed, close to rivers or in rural areas. Mice love chocolate and the warm so you'll need to make sure your shop is rodent proof!

You'll need a place to store stock that's off floor level, although ideally you'll want as much stock out on display as possible. You won't necessarily need an in shop toilet or hand-wash but you should have access to one.

If you decide at a later date to sell ice creams these will need to be pre-packaged.

You will need a method of ensuring your shop maintains the chocolates at ambient storage temperature. In our opinion the best way to achieve this is a window out of direct sunlight and modern air conditioning.

Selling loose chocolates plus other food

If you're planning to repackage loose items such as fresh Chocolates, sell cakes, run a café, or potentially scoop ice cream then your layout requirements are more extensive, but not too complicated.

You'll need access to a toilet (not necessarily on your premises) If you have a toilet it will need extraction and a separate lobby to prevent direct opening onto food preparation or customer facing areas.

You'll need a separate hand-wash and washing up area. This could be two separate bowls in the same sink. They will need a hot water supply, soap dispenser and means of drying your hands. You might want to consider a separate dish-washer or glass washer.

We ran our ancillary café with three indoor tables with 9 seats and three outdoor tables. We served tea, coffee and hot chocolate, fresh chocolates and a small cake selection. For this we had a double bowl sink in the back of house area and a small commercial glass washer which we used as a dishwasher. We used an inexpensive water heater above our hand wash, though these tended to need replacing every couple of years. We also had a separate hand wash in the toilet area.

Illustration

19: Creating the back of house area- a false wall built here - the upside down bath-tub isn't ours!

You'll need plumbing and drainage for all of these items. From experience have plenty of access points built into your sink and glass washer drainage. Cocoa butter is a solid at room temperature and drains can easily clog where your cold water drains and meets glass washer drainage!

Chocolates and cakes are *relatively* low risk food items. They generally contain enough sugar and fat to make bacterial growth very slow and cakes tend to be eaten within a very short period after being made. Note we are talking about simple ambient based cakes such as brownies and sponges, not fresh cream filled cakes, patisserie or custard tarts!

So the biggest risk to chocolates and cakes on ambient display is cross-contamination. For this you will want to consider covers and sneeze screens. However it is a point for discussion. In our shop we wanted a pick your own chocolate counter where the customer could make their own selection. Our counter was high and set back, but accessible. There was a small sneeze screen but the chocolates were essentially accessible. We argued that they were low risk items with a fast turnover and there was no need to cover them. We did cover our cakes with glass domes.

Illustration

20: An early version of our fresh chocolate counter with small sneeze screen

Chocolates do not enjoy being refrigerated! They tend to attract condensation, ruining the surface finish, causing unsightly sugar bloom and creating a breeding ground for bacteria.

If you decide to go for a refrigerated unit, a wine chiller is a much more appropriate temperature than a deli counter. We air conditioned our shop rather than opt for a refrigerated chocolate display cabinet. This worked well and our shop was always cool in the summer. I remember one summer a Japanese tourist and family walking in and standing to cool in front of the air conditioning as the street baked in the sun commenting that we were the only cool shop.

If you are considering patisserie items you will need a separate, colder refrigerated display cabinet for patisserie. Much patisserie is supplied frozen and then defrosted on the day. This is the model a well known high street Patisserie chain uses for example.

Patisserie, once defrosted, is a high risk food product It needs considered handling, storage and stock rotation.

You could use a small freezer or the storage compartment of an Ice Cream scooping freezer for patisserie storage, as long as it retains a stable temperature of -18c or colder.

It's worth mentioning that the serving part of an ice cream scooping freezer operates at a higher temperature than needed for storage. Macaroons freeze very well and defrost within 15 minutes, so can be topped up as needed – very useful!

So to recap, You'll need back of house areas for...

- Washing hands and crockery if appropriate
- storage of cleaning chemicals and equipment (with a simple chemical storage register Control of Substances Hazardous to Health (COSHH)
- storage of clean equipment and crockery
- food and other waste disposal
- secure staff area to hang coats, bags and aprons
- storage for ambient chocolate items
- storage for frozen or refrigerated stock

Shop flooring, shelving and back of house areas need to be washable and durable. When considering your layout think about daily cleaning needs and how you'll stack any tables or chairs at night to allow easy cleaning when all you really want to do is get home.

If in doubt contact Environmental health. They are (currently at the time of writing) a free service and can help you avoid costly mistakes in planning and layout if you involve them from the start. **It is worth** mentioning that officers in Environmental health and Trading standards are free to interpret the law as they see fit.

This means that just because you saw a shop with an open chocolate counter in Yorkshire, it doesn't necessarily mean that the officer in Buckinghamshire will concur and allow you to do the same!

SHOP DESIGN ON A SHOE STRING

So you've decided on a shop, but how are you going to fit it out?

It will probably surprise you that a shop can be presented to rent to you in any state from a completely empty shell to a finished shop unit almost ready to move in.

If the shop is a new build then you are more likely to be presented with a shop in bare bones format. Electricity installation will probably be what they call first fix and walls and floors may be finished to varying standards. You'll need to negotiate carefully with your landlords to check just what state you'll receive the unit in and though it's a long way away, check what state it needs to be in when you eventually end the lease in case this affects how you fit out the unit. Units are often presented in this way to allow teams of shop fitters to implement your 'merchandising vision'. This can be daunting as an independent if you've never done this kind of fit out!

21: Fitting out a shop from a shell can be a daunting task

Some landlords are recognising this and putting new units that are fitted to a clean standard that could potentially be moved into with minimal or no building work. These units also have potential as pop-up shop lets.

What if I have to start with a bare shell?

If you're moving into a new set of units you may have access to shop fitters working on other units. This was the position we found ourselves in with our Cirencester shop. We had an idea of what we needed...

- Sumptuous chocolate counter for loose chocolates

- Central Chocolate merchandising podium for pre-packaged items

- Seating and tables for customers to enjoy hot drinks

- Staff toilet and hand wash

- Back of house area with storage, dishwasher and washing up area

- Behind counter coffee and hot chocolate machine area plus under counter storage

- Lighting
- Till and payment area
- Window display unit
- Small back of house night safe
- Minimal budget for shop fitting!

We had no shop designer though Diana was very artistic. We discovered an incredibly useful free tool – Google Sketchup. This brilliant tool allows you to draw a footprint of your shop and then drag it up into a 3D model. There are libraries of tables, chairs and other items and it is easy to construct simple 3D shapes from squares and circles. Without too much effort we had produced a simple layout that allowed us to visualise the shop and show it to the shop fitters to talk about pricing.

Illustration

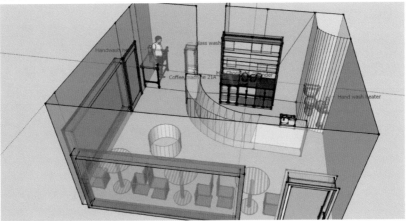

22: Free tools like Google Sketchup allow you to quickly visualise how your shop might look

The shop next door to us was to be the showcase for a new type of shop for a well established perfume and soap specialist. I recall the day we walked into the shop-fitters temporary office and were shown the beautiful 3D CAD generated drawings of the shop next door with their 50k budget. Our A4 printed Sketchup model was underneath it with a hand drawn exclamation mark next to it! We felt a little inadequate but stuck to our guns.

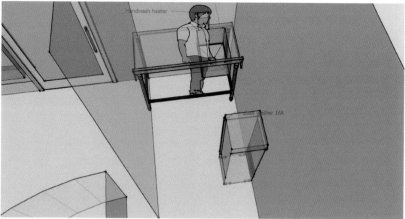

23: Planning the back of house area

Three years later the shop next door sadly closed as the group went bankrupt, **spending a fortune on shop fitting is no guarantee of success.**

There are a few companies who offer off the shelf shop fitting equipment. They're usually quite expensive and often don't look that good. Whilst you should research and consider these for pricing or planning, you can do as well looking on eBay or shops such as Ikea for cheaper alternatives.

If you think of Harvey Nichols food hall for example you'll probably think of luxury. However if you look closely at the shop fittings for the most part they are stark stainless wire shelves. It is the way the stock is merchandised, lighting and signage that really make the difference.

For this pop-up shop in Bath we temporarily re-used our wire frame ingredients racks, they were not dissimilar to those used by Harvey Nichols at the time. A display banner at the back is used to add instant but temporary branding and shield an unfinished area of the shop.

24: For a pop-up shop you'll want to spend minimal money on shop fitting

For our Cirencester shop after some negotiation with our landlords it was agreed that they would pay for the toilet installation and we would pay for the false wall we needed for the back of house area, spot lighting, decorating, electrical installation needed for sockets, coffee machine, dishwasher and plumbing.

As we had access to shop fitters we also talked through making a bespoke chocolate counter, central display unit and window display unit with storage. This proved to be a good move as though bespoke the use of a wood veneer produced beautiful and hard wearing units that were equivalent pricing to low end shop fit catalogue units even with a bespoke glass counter top!

25: *Our bespoke chocolate counter was as cheap as some off the shelf units*

We used a simple spread sheet to price up the fit out - included in the Business Plan appendix as an example. We worked on a budget of £12,000.

Diana decided that a statement feature of the shop would be an elaborate crystal chandelier and this took several hundred pounds from our budget but proved to be worth it as it really made the shop look special and was a great visual attraction.

We needed a cool surface to keep the chocolates on and marble or granite is perfect for this. So we had our local kitchen granite worktop company cut 25cm 10cm thick granite slabs that we could use as a base display layer for chocolates in our custom cabinet. We also had them cut three table top sized pieces of the same granite that could be fixed to commercial table legs using a special cement by our shop fitters.

We really wanted to buy some elaborate customer chairs but in the end our budget was too stretched for this and so we opted for a budget wooden option that were functional and fitted in with the overall appearance.

71

26: Our children test out our chairs - these were a compromise on budget. The bespoke wallpaper gives the air of a luxury chocolate shop connected to cocoa growers

TIP You must budget for cash flow in the early months of your shop. If you blow everything on shop fitting you could run out of cash soon after your shop opens!

We opted for a new and efficient air conditioning unit that could both heat and cool our shop. This proved a good move and reduced electricity bills in the long run. It was also able to dehumidify the shop on humid days.

27: Air conditioning is installed at the rear of the shop. The external unit was up the stairs, under the floor of the flat above and on the service roof!

For the rear wall we found a Scottish company that could custom print photos onto wallpaper. We were able to create a large mural with cocoa pods using a stock image that was perfect for a chocolate shop. The rest of the walls were plastered and finished in a scrub-able paint.

For our coffee machine we trawled eBay as new ones were very expensive. We took advice from local Bristol Coffee roaster Brian Wogan who had come highly recommended, and eventually settled on an old Cimbali Italian machine which we were told by Brian was a well made brand. It needed careful servicing internally and set up by Brian Wogan, but proved to be a good machine that made excellent coffee.

28: Testing out the newly installed Coffee machine

Be careful choosing coffee machines and take advice from your chosen coffee roaster. They are pressurised machines that can explode and usually need to be noted on insurance policies and serviced regularly.

We purchased a second hand hot chocolate machine also from eBay. These machines are quite simple, they feature a Bain-Marie to keep the hot chocolate at temperature and a rotating paddle that churns the chocolate keeping it emulsified together. They are very useful if you plan to serve hot chocolate, but not absolutely essential as you can use the frothing arm of your coffee machine. But they do save time if you plan to serve a lot of hot chocolate - well you are a chocolate shop!

Tills and payment systems

Without a means of taking money your shop wouldn't really function very well! Whilst cash boxes work well for market situations you'll need something a little more sophisticated for your shop.

Till systems vary hugely from the very simple that can be picked up for around £90 and are little more than a cash-box and electronic calculator, to sophisticated touch screen devices with full stock management that can be remotely accessed.

This is another area you'll most likely have to make some compromise in choice. For our shop we settled on a Samsung till that cost just over £200. It had built in stock control but this was accessed by the built in printer. Programming was similarly by a series of a key strokes. In hindsight it was one of the areas I wish we had more to spend as we could never extract the detailed sales reports we really needed. However it was sufficient to run a shop and manually transfer to a spreadsheet, a job delegated to our shop manager.

We've included some more detailed information on till systems in the appendix - though a stiff cup of coffee may be needed first!

How do I take card payments?

Taking card payments is essential for all shops these days. Fortunately in the last couple of years it's become a lot easier with many new low cost card payment terminals coming on the market.

The traditional payment route requires what is known as a Merchant Account. This is a separate bank account from your normal day to day bank account that you will need to apply for. Perhaps surprisingly this isn't as straight forward as you might think largely because the merchant banks are worried about fraud. Fortunately chocolates and cakes etc. are relatively low transaction costs so the fraud risk is much lower than someone selling a car for example. Well known merchant accounts include World Pay and Lloyds Cardnet.

They will charge you for the privilege of having the account, for so called PCI checks and also per transaction based on a negotiable rate. Typically a debit card is a fixed fee - say 20p per transaction, whilst a credit card is a fixed fee plus a %, say 2%. On top of all this you'll need to either buy a very expensive card terminal - typically £600+ or hire one on a 2 year contract. The terminals are usually locked to a particular merchant account so you can't easily buy them second hand.

If you have high turnover these machines can save you money on the debit card transactions but you do need to add it all up and do some spreadsheet projections.

They usually come with a built in thermal printer.

So at the end of the day when cashing up you would run a Z report (an end of day sales total – see till systems appendix) on your card machine, and if not linked to your till, cross check against the card takings recorded in the till. We'll cover this more in day to day running procedures.

More recently companies such as iZettle and PayPal have introduced low cost card terminals and all in one merchant accounts that have greatly simplified the process.

The terminals can be purchased for around £50 and whilst not as substantial as the traditional ones, can be more up to date in terms of technology, supporting contactless, Apple Pay etc.

The izettle or Paypal merchant account application is much more straight forward. The only issue you might find is the need to personally underwrite the account if you have no trading history. This isn't as bad as it sounds as the risk of fraud is relatively low due to the low average transaction value. If somebody walks in off the street and wants to buy the entire contents of your shop by credit card – be wary!

Paypal and izettle terminals usually require connectivity through your mobile phone and have an associated App. We've used izettle and found it to be excellent. The terminals are pretty much the same between izettle and PayPal so it's really down to fee structures and who you prefer. They usually have a sliding %fee that might start at 3% and drops to 1.5% as you pass monthly sales thresholds. So for debit card transactions it can work out more expensive than a traditional terminal. But it could be worth starting this way and then switching to a more traditional terminal once you've worked out your sales volumes and how much you're paying.

The apps also have simple inventory tracking and can be used to track cash sales. So whilst not perfect you could use a simpler till system and use this app to record sales. They don't use 'Z reports' and automatically add up the daily sales. Altogether much easier to buy, set up and use than the traditional providers.

TIP Why not start off with an izettle or Paypal terminal for card payments. You can switch to a more expensive system if sales warrant it at a later date.

One more thing - don't put in place a minimum card payment or charge for card transactions. Take the hit! Everybody pays by card these days and many people don't carry cash, so it's better for customer relations to work the fees into your own margins.

CHOOSING A SHOP NAME

One of the most exciting aspects of opening a new shop is choosing your shop name. A catchy or memorable name in keeping with your business will be the cornerstone of your brand. As you will soon see from a quick web search there are many chocolate shops using variations of 'choco', 'cocoa', 'cacao', and 'chocolates'. So it can be quite hard to be original! When you've thought of names for your shop run it by as many independent people as you can as you'll have to live with it for a long time. There are also a few legal things to check.

When you choose a name for your business you need to make sure you won't be infringing another company's intellectual property (IP).

To check this do a trademark search on IPO.gov.uk for your chosen name. You may need to check the chocolate & confectionery based categories as well as retail categories. If you're a small shop people won't necessarily worry or notice until customer confusion occurs. Clearly if your name is John Lewis and you call your shop John Lewis's Chocolate Shop you might cause people confusion and ultimately have to change your shop name. So it's best to do this from the start and even pay the £200 to register your own trademark.

You may also want to perform a web domain search to see if someone is using the name or a variation. The trademark is the most important as a web domain has no legal power. But it would be nice to have both free so you can register both at once and secure your future. You might similarly want to check social media and take out free accounts in your chosen name or as close as you can to it.

Branding – Shop Signage

You'll want to proudly display your shop name on the front of your shop and this might be the first point at which you consider branding and logos. Branding is too large a subject to go into detail here. But in a nutshell the way you visually present your shop name in combinations of font, colour and pictorial representation gives your potential customers both direct and subliminal clues as to what kind of business you are.

For example **Times New Roman** font gives a feel of tradition and stability. Whereas Curlz MT is fun and quirky. On that note avoid the Curlz font beloved of cup cake shops – it's not a good choice on so many levels and will undermine all other attempts to make your shop look professional! In the extreme brands such as Waitrose have designed their own font that is carried across all products, signage and literature giving a cohesive look and brand identity.

If at this point your eyes are glazing over - don't panic! You don't need to spend an absolute fortune on branding, but you do need a logo that looks professional, is in character with your brand, and carries across from your shop front to print advertising to your website.

If money is tight (as it most likely will be) you might want to consider a local independent graphic designer or use websites such as designcrowd.co.uk* that allow you to get a number of designers to pitch ideas to a budget. *We have no personal experience of this website.

The best logos are usually the simplest and read well in black and white – think of the BBC for example. You'll have to live with your logo for many years so it's one of those areas that is worth allocating a budget for as it can be reused throughout your business – business cards, menus, gift tags, stickers, chocolate box lids.

And.... yes your brother, cousin, friend down the pub may have a talented artistic 16 year old son or daughter who's a whizz on the computer, but they won't have to live with your logo for ten years, so politely decline and use a professional designer if you can or stick to a simple font that you use consistently.

Getting the sign made

Once you have your shop name and logo you'll need to get your sign made. It's likely that there will be some limitations on signage location particularly if you are in a conservation area. So check council plans as to location and size of allowed signage. You may also want to get a moveable 'A' board made at the same time allowing you to advertise daily specials. In our experience shop sign writers and makers aren't the fastest people to mobilise so plan this in before you intend to open!

FINDING SUPPLIERS

How do you go about finding suppliers?

Fortunately in this day of the internet finding suppliers is a lot easier than it used to be. A simple google search for 'Wholesale chocolates' will turn up a list of potential suppliers. You can also contact fine food organisations such as the Guild of Fine Food or Taste of the West and they will be happy to supply you a list of their producer members.

Potential suppliers could be...

- Wholesale Cash and Carry – more suited to mass produced items
- Fine Food Wholesale distributors that deliver
- Direct purchase from small producers – such as ourselves Lick the Spoon!

What's the difference between buying from a distributor and buying direct?

A distributor will collate a number of suppliers into one catalogue often supplemented with seasonal catalogues. The advantage they have is you can combine several different suppliers into one purchase order. Many include sundry items such as napkins, sugar cubes, Ice Cream cones, disposable coffee cups, cleaning items and anything else you can think of needed for day to day running. So it's likely you'll need at least one distributor for items like these and preferably one with a local delivery route.

All Wholesale distributors will add a markup of 15-25% on the manufacturers price. They have to do this or they won't make a profit! However they won't always be a higher price than buying direct as manufacturers will usually offer distributors a lower price for the advantages of delivering in bulk. Some manufacturers don't sell direct and others price such that it is actually cheaper to buy from a distributor to encourage you to do so.

The only disadvantage of buying from a distributor is that you're more likely to come across mass produced goods. So you need to decide your customer base and the tone you want to set for your shop.

What about buying direct?

Buying direct will give you the opportunity to source direct from the producer and also tell the story of the product as well as offering something unique. The disadvantages may be a limited range making it difficult to meet minimum orders and possibly a longer lead time from small producers.

It makes sense to have a few potential sources for your chocolate products to limit your risk.

As a new business when approaching suppliers it's wise to have as much information as possible available to identify yourselves as a business.

As a wholesale supplier ourselves in the run up to Christmas we get many people approach us for wholesale chocolates with only a tenuous link to a business. We get many emails such as 'I'm thinking of opening a chocolate shop, please send me your catalogue and samples – walterwhite@gmail.com'

Not surprisingly we ask for more information in these circumstances. It usually helps to have a business email, some information on your shop, some way of identifying you as a retail business and not a competitor or simply trying to buy wholesale chocolates for Christmas presents!

STAFFING YOUR SHOP

So you're all set to go, you've fitted out your shop, sourced your chocolates, and possibly Ice cream, coffee, tea, hot chocolate and a range of patisserie or cakes. How do you staff your shop?

Staffing is probably one of the biggest headaches any small business owner will tell you. Particularly with a retail shop or café where you need to be open potentially every day. If you over staff you have staff twiddling their thumbs, if you under staff service levels fall and if it continues so do customers. Somebody calls in sick at short notice and you may have to cover on your day off. It's really hard!

When we were first considering staffing we took some advice from the federation of master bakers. A lovely lady who worked there had previously run a café and bakery and suggested that two part time shop managers had worked well for them. We took this onboard and though our shop was small we had the two shop manager model in mind. As we had only just opened our production facility the month before and had grand plans to open a network of shops we had decided right from the start that neither of us would be rota'd in to running the shop. With hindsight a mistake!

We ended up employing a full time shop manager, a part time shop manager, and a full time shop assistant. I'm sure that even looking on paper you can see that this was a little unbalanced! We also had in our mind that we were never going to employ 16 year old Saturday staff. We were going to offer the highest levels of service and not be one of those shops with bored Saturday teenagers. Again a mistake we were to eventually rectify. We also initially only planned to open Monday to Saturday and close on Sundays.

As we threw ourselves into running the shop over the first two years we realised that we had made several mistakes.

Firstly we needed to open Sundays. We were in a touristic town and though most of our competition closed on a Sunday it was a missed opportunity. People would meander round the town with nothing to do and nowhere to eat or drink. So we sat down with our three shop staff and they were good enough to agree to cover the Sundays between them on a new rota. There are hardly any retailers these days that can afford to cover rent and rates without opening seven days a week and most people do their shopping at the weekends.

Harsh Truth - You'll most likely need to open 7 days a week

We also realised that we had over-staffed in the week. A quiet Monday didn't need two members of staff and one could cope. Fortunately things sorted themselves out. After a year our full time shop manager left to further her career and our part time manager left to have a baby.

This left our shop assistant who had narrowly missed out on the shop managers job at the first interview and had proven herself to be incredibly reliable and trustworthy.

So after two years we had one full time shop manager five days a week and I myself worked three days with an overlap. Lunchtimes were a little difficult but we accepted that closing the shop for half an hour with a sign outside of the main lunchtime Rush was acceptable.

We also rapidly changed our mind on 16 year old assistants. Whilst the weekdays could be managed with just one person most of the time Saturdays were very busy and sometimes needed three people to keep on top of clearing tables, serving Ice Creams and chocolates. It turned out a ready supply of six formers and college students would appear in the shop with a CV and we started to employ them on a casual basis for Saturdays and sometimes Sundays in the summer. We affectionately called them 'Teaspoons' for Trainee Lick the Spoons. They were usually happy to work on a flexible rota allowing time off and were preparing to go to University. We found them to be polite, motivated and perfect for Saturdays. It was also easy to recruit new Saturday staff when they left for University via a sign in the window.

We found that rather than a formal interview it was better to invite them in to work for a couple of hours, see how they interacted with customers and how confident they were.

We also learnt to avoid mothers who would drop in and try and secure a job for their son or daughter. The son or daughter inevitably were either incredibly shy or didn't really want a job.

The biggest mistake we made was to not work in the shop ourself from the start. We had never run a shop before so we set it up based on the experience we thought our customers wanted. Whilst this was pretty close as Diana had worked in hospitality for some of the finest restaurants and hotels. We missed the day to day details of how customers were experiencing our shop. Though lots of information was getting passed back to us, as we weren't experiencing it we didn't act on it as quickly as we should have done. For example, many of the customers visiting our shop were older and wanted more traditional chocolates such as Rose and Violet creams. We dismissed this initially -

that wasn't our style. Eventually we relented and they have been a staple ever since. Many small details were missed like this.

More importantly without being in the shop at the start we had no idea how busy the shop actually was and consequently how many staff we needed on particular days. How much the weather affected sales. If it rains in the morning people stay home. If it's sunny in the morning and rains at lunchtime the shop would sometimes get stampeded. We would close the shop at 4 on a Sunday but this was the time when a rush would occur of people wanting Ice creams before they finish their day. Shops are always busier on payday weekend. All of these little variations can only be seen when you're working in a shop. So at first it makes sense to overlap and try and see all of the days. Otherwise variations in takings will confuse you or even make you suspicious.

Harsh Truth - You need to be in the shop yourself for the first few months at least

So at first work in the shop yourself as much as possible. If it's a small shop you may need to do this anyway as it may not support multiple staff as profits will be low once wages are taken out. Don't over staff to start off with. Try and take on assistants with a flexible contract. Zero hours contracts have a lot of bad publicity for understandable reasons but once you enter the retail arena you realise the difficulty of covering all opening hours and maintaining your sanity is challenging. We found guaranteeing a minimum number of hours worked well e.g. 16 hours minimum per week with flexibility. This was backed up with casual Saturday staff who didn't mind the flexibility. Certainly don't limit yourself on working days or back yourself into a corner until you know what is needed for your shop. But be prepared there will undoubtedly be times when you get a sick call and you have to cover on your Saturday off.

Legal Aspects of taking on Staff

There are a few legal aspects to taking on staff that you need to be aware of. In the UK the https://www.gov.uk/browse/business website should be your first port of call with lots of help and advice, but you can also find advice from your local Chambers of Commerce who may have one day courses on offer. Trade bodies such as the Guild of Fine Food, The Federation of Small Businesses, Taste of the West and ACAS can also offer advice and resources.

Here is a brief summary...

You will need to...

- Register with HMRC as an employer

- Have employers liability insurance – usually part of a combined retail insurance policy

- Put in place simple Health and Safety, fire plan, risk assesment and other policies on sick pay, leave etc

- Give your employees a statement of employment and a simple offer letter contract stating the main terms of employment pay, working hours etc. (Try not to box yourself in too much with working hours until you know your shop requirements)

- Pay your employees and pay any tax and national insurance due on their behalf (PAYE) together with online HMRC filing

- Consider their eligibility for a pension scheme. The government NEST scheme is a good default option.

If all of that sounds like a lot, well, it is... but it's not quite as bad as it sounds!

For payroll you could use an accountant who will handle all of that for you, and add in for your accounts package, or a standalone package such as Moneysoft Payroll manager costing around £60 per year.

For the first couple of years we used an accountant to run our payroll. However when we switched accountancy firms our new accountant suggested we could do it ourself.

I used Moneysoft Payroll manager which is an excellent and incredibly easy to use package. It will do all of your online filing, generate payslips, keep track of holidays and sickness and pension enrollment. So whilst it's another thing on the seemingly long list of admin keeping you away from your customers, with a little set up help from your accountant it could save you money and give you flexibility in the long run. More on accounts later.

Recently I moved from Moneysoft to a payroll add in on our Xero accounts package. I have to say Moneysoft was so much easier to use though it's not cloud based.

We've also found ACAS are excellent for impartial advice when those tricky staff situations occasionally arise. We started a staff handbook and each time some circumstance occurred we hadn't thought of ... a friends pet octopus dies suddenly for example, we'd check out as best we could the legal aspects and then write a section in the handbook!

Pricing your Chocolates

There is no one size fits all magic rule to pricing your chocolates, but there are some tried and tested principles you can use.

Whilst your suppliers may offer a Recommended Retail Price or RRP, in the UK you are free to sell at whatever price wish.

But clearly there are some rules that you need to apply. Firstly your shop will have costs that you need to cover in order to make a profit.

These are...

- **Fixed costs** – annual rent, service charge, business rates, electricity, water and staff wages*

- **Variable costs** – the cost of buying the goods from your suppliers, and any associated costs that increase as you sell more items*

*Whilst your shop staff could be considered a fixed cost it may be that if you are serving lots of tea and coffee and need to take on more staff as sales ramp up to clear tables etc, that these might be considered a variable cost. You may consider a split of management as overheads or fixed costs and serving staff as variable costs.

So as a simple example...

My Chocolate Shop		
	Rent	10,000 PA
	Service Charge	1000 PA
	Electricity	1000 PA
	Water	750 PA
	Staff	20,250 PA
Total Fixed Costs		**33,000 PA**

My Chocolate Shop sells chocolate bars which it purchases at £1 each

Variable Costs £1 per bar

My Chocolate Shop prices the bars at a selling price of **£2** and sells **40,000** per year

My chocolate shop **Turnover** = 40,000 x £2 = £80,000 Per Annum (PA)

My chocolate shop **Gross Profit** = 40,000 x (£2 -£1) = £40,000

Gross profit is a company's total total sales minus the cost of goods sold

My chocolate shop **Net Profit** = £40,000 - £33,000 = £7000 PA

Net Profit - the actual profit after working expenses not included in the calculation of gross profit have been paid.

A very simple example but illustrates the concept of Turnover, Gross Profit, Net profit, Fixed and Variable costs.

Another term you may come across is Gross Profit Margin often shortened to Profit Margin.

Gross Margin % = (Retail selling Price – Wholesale price to you)/ Retail Selling Price x 100

In this example Gross Profit Margin = (£2 - £1)/£2 x100 = 0.5 x 100 = 50%

This is actually a classic pricing model that you can work to. Note all prices here are excluding VAT. Though in reality your supplier will most likely be VAT registered and you initially won't be.

Typically you should aim to make an average 50% gross profit margin. This is sometimes referred to as Keystone pricing. Essentially with a keystone pricing model you double the cost price to create your retail selling price.

If you buy from a distributor they will add their own margin on top of the supplier's price, so you may need to opt for a smaller margin of 35% in order to sell at the manufacturer's RRP. In the UK manufacturers can suggest retail prices but you are free by law to sell at any price you like. So in theory you could always make a 50% gross profit on every product. But it depends what you're selling, where else it is available and if your customer base is willing to pay that price for the product.

Large department stores typically aim to price at above the 50% margin rate. Discounters will price at much less than the rate aiming for a large turnover. So there is no hard and fast pricing rule but as you're unlikely to have bulk buying capability your purchasing and pricing should reflect your niche.

Looking at the simple example it should also leap out at you that selling 40,000 chocolate bars a year equates to an average of over a 100 a day even if you open every single day of the year! This is quite a lot and is probably more than your local supermarket will sell of specialist bars in a given day!

In the Business plan shown in the appendix we show how you can experiment with different product mixes and up-sells to achieve your daily targets.

When you buy pre-packaged retail items from a supplier you are paying for their time to pack the goods and their profit on top of that.

If you add loose unpackaged items into your product mix – a fresh chocolate counter, tea, coffee, Ice Cream sundaes for example, you will be supplying the labour with your shop staff and should therefore carry a higher gross profit margin for yourself.

As an example...

Loose chocolates – as an example say on average 30p per chocolate.

12 chocolates cost price £3.60

Flat packed chocolate box £1

Total cost price £4-60 *

Selling Price £12 (assume you're not VAT rated)

Gross Margin = (£12 - £4-60) = £7.40 / £12 x 100 = 61%

* your supplier may charge you VAT – not included for this simple example.

Of course if you took this to extremes and had no pre-packaged items you would effectively become the manufacturer and your staff costs would be higher. But a product mix that makes maximum use of your staff down time, making up flat pack chocolate boxes for example, will help maximise your profitability.

In our experience it *is* possible to run a small chocolate shop *and* make enough *profit* to make a living, but you will need to work hard at it as do all modern retail stores.

A TYPICAL DAY IN A CHOCOLATE SHOP

There's no guarantee your day will be anything like this of course. But here's how a typical day in our shop would pan out when working on my own on a weekday.

I would arrive in town from my 20 mile drive around 8-15am, park in the out of town low cost car park and walk into town. If I had worked the day before I would know whether milk was needed and would buy milk on the way. (We had considered a delivery round but it would have meant leaving the milk outside for a couple of hours as we had no easy place to put it and deliveries were early). I would also buy sandwiches for my own lunch. I usually stayed open through lunch grabbing a bite to eat when I could, though your staff will have legal entitlement to a lunch break. It will be almost impossible to employ someone just to cover lunch breaks so it's easier to have a 'gone for lunch' or 'back in half hour' notice if your staff are working alone.

I'd open the shop and turn on the coffee machine so that it could reach temperature before the first customers arrived, closing the door behind me and keeping lights off at this point as I knew from experience that if I started to sell I'd never get set up properly.

Next I would read any notes left on how the previous day went and then open the small back of house safe (you will need a small shop safe) to retrieve the till float and any money that needed to be banked. I would also check the previous day's takings. After a year we also kept the previous year's takings record so we had an approximate target for the day.

The till was always switched off at night and left with the drawer empty and open.

I would then put the till float back into the till, it was typically £100. I cannot stress how important it is if you have multiple staff to carefully check floats and till takings. If it was my first day in I would check the milk in the fridge, and dash to the bank and shop to buy milk, bank the previous day's takings and get change needed for the till. Even if we had a really quiet previous day we had a policy of always banking the takings. It really helps with bank reconciliation in your accounts package, and, if any money is unexplained it is so much easier to pin-point when it went wrong and who was working on that day.

On return to the shop I would put the change in the till, apron on, wash hands, switch on music, switch on the glass washer so it started to heat. Commercial dishwashers and glass washers use a continuously heated water reservoir so they can cycle through quicker but it takes 10 minutes to heat up. The shop doors were opened and I put the folded outside tables and chairs outside. We brought these into the shop each night. I would put out menus and sugar bowls and the A board and of course switch the lights on. We usually opened at 9-30 weekdays.

I would check and record fridge temperatures, the hot chocolate record and see if there was a refrigerated batch or whether I needed to make new. I would then heat it up using the coffee machine steam wand which took several minutes before pouring it into the hot chocolate machine and fitting the paddle so it was kept hot and agitated for the day. By this point of course we may have had customers, so I always stopped whatever I was doing to acknowledge and serve people and often they were regulars who I would pass the time of day with.

In the Ice cream months I would remove the covers from the Ice Cream tubs, check if any needed replacing with the stored tubs and replace if necessary. It was always better to keep these full and ball up any Ice cream in an almost empty tub and put it onto a full tub. I'd fill the Ice cream scoop jug with water and a dash of sterilising fluid and put fresh cones ready to go. If it looked like a hot day I'd wheel the freezer outside the shop and put on a money belt. It was a small enough shop that this always increased takings on hot days. I would usually also polish the freezer glass. For me if we didn't have a customer in the shop then I wanted it to be absolutely perfectly gleaming when they did walk in.

I'd then check the chocolate display working my way through replenishing chocolates, checking best before dates to make sure we didn't miss any and polishing any Perspex sheets that didn't look spotless. Flat pack boxes were folded so there was always some stock to go.

Then in between customers I would work through a cleaning schedule that we maintained. You always notice more when it's your own shop, so if I hadn't been in for a few days I'd usually end up dusting skirting boards and tidying back of house.

When you have a shop you realise that like buses customers always turn up all at once. Often around lunch time, or simply the sight of someone else in the shop will entice them in. So I always acknowledged customers, smiled and said hello, but worked in sequence through the customers without trying to multi-task. Once early on I had tried to combine multiple drink orders from different customers. I simply got in a mess if I didn't complete one order and go on to the next.

The self service counter really helped here and regular customers would often walk in, pick up a plate and start making their chocolate selection whilst I served other customers with drinks.

In between serving customers tables would be cleared and the glass washer loaded to ensure we didn't run out of clean crockery, though we had a good reserve, but not much space to store dirty dishes. I'd usually grab lunch between customers and try not to be noticed eating.

Most of the day was spent serving and cleaning and it's pretty tiring on your own. I never had a seat behind the till and still never sit down if I'm selling. There's nothing worse than seeing a bored shop assistant on a stool behind the till staring at their phone.

Around 4-30 I would empty out the hot chocolate into a jug and if it was able to be refrigerated I would put it to cool before putting in the fridge. 4-45 and I would clean the coffee machine and then turn it off. Final dishes would be washed and any rubbish and recycling gathered. At 5pm I would turn the lights off, bring outside tables and chairs in, cover any cakes, cover the Ice cream freezer tubs, drain the dishwasher, put all of the tables and chairs up and mop the floor. I would then cash up the till and card machine firstly with a till X report, and then a Z report to clear the totals (see appendix on tills if this makes no sense!). I would then Z report the card machine to zero the totals for the next day.

The cash takings would be taken and put into the safe to bank, the card machine receipts were put in an envelope and the total cash and card takings for that day written on the front. These would be collated weekly for accounting. The till £100 float was then carefully counted and put separately into the safe and a note for next day written. If I was lucky I would shut the shop at 5-30 and head home putting the rubbish in the designated bin area on the way.

Of course it was my shop and if there were lots of customers I would stay open longer. But this was sometimes diminishing returns and you'd never get home.

It was hard work but I did enjoy meeting people and telling them about our chocolates and people came from all over the world to visit! We gained a reputation for excellence and were listed in both Time Out and Lonely Planet guides in the top ten places to visit in the Cotswolds!

MARKETING YOUR SHOP

So you're about to open your shop - how do you make sure people will come and visit?

I have to admit that with hindsight the one time I would be tempted to advertise is when you first open. We've always avoided paid advertising unless we felt it absolutely necessary to achieve a goal and it's possible to achieve an enormous amount of free PR. As a chocolate shop you'll find this much easier than say a cling film company - everyone loves a good chocolate story!

But when you first open you will have ploughed a lot of start up money in and will need to start recouping it, so advertising with local papers at this point might well reap rewards. You'll probably also be offered the advertorial - a form of write up that reads like a journalistic article but is actually a form of paid advertising.

So what can I do for free or minimal spend?

Firstly if you have time you should plan in a website to coincide with your launch or ideally before your launch. A website is vital these days and you'll miss lots of potential customers without one.

CREATING A WEBSITE

We could write a whole other book on this, but here are a couple of solutions.

Branding

Firstly you don't need to spend an absolute fortune on branding but you do need a logo that looks professional, is in character with your brand, and carries across from your shop front to print advertising to your website.

Secondly you need some great photographs, ideally of your shop! You can pay a local photographer to do this for half a day and these will also be useful for Press Releases and advertising. In the meantime you could use a nice licensed chocolate image purchased for a small amount from somewhere like Shutterstock (don't just pinch one from google images it will be someone else's copyright).

Creating the Website

A couple of possible solutions are managed solutions such as Shopify, and your own hosted solution such as Wordpress.

Managed solution such as Shopify – this is probably the simplest form but locks you in to a specific platform with a monthly fee. Platforms such as Shopify have a range of great looking templates that instantly give you a professional look. They also take care of web hosting, secure payments when you want to sell online and site security issues. The downside is you may come across a functional requirement that isn't currently available and you're tied in to monthly fees with no easy way to switch should you want to.

Wordpress – I'm a huge fan of Wordpress, currently something like 25% of all websites are Wordpress based sites and over 30% of all ecommerce sites use Woocommerce running on Wordpress. Wordpress started as a free blogging platform created using the open source model. It is now has a huge community world wide. It's visual appearance or look is based on 'themes' of which there are 1000's. Functionality over and above blogging is added through plugins of which there are also 1000's. You will need a hosting company for your Wordpress website or use a free hosting on Wordpress.com. The advantages of Wordpress are its huge community, it's largely free, is almost infinitely expandable, and you own the site.

For web hosting companies I would recommend Clook in the UK for small sites and Cloudways for more complex websites.

The disadvantages of Wordpress are its popularity and ease of adding capabilities or functionality via bits of software called plugins make it is prone to hacker attacks. So you'll need to think about security from the start. With this in mind it's better to chose a well supported paid 'theme' and choose plugins carefully.

So if you're a complete technophobe choose something like Shopify, if you'd prefer to own the site and take more control yourself use Wordpress.

You'll want a web domain for your site. This can be done through a domain reselling company like easily.co.uk for nominal amounts of money. Avoid paying huge amounts of money to speculators who've parked domain names, it's far less relevant these days and it's what you do with the site that will affect how it is displayed in Google.

Ok so you've put up a simple website, how do you tell the world about it?

GOOGLE

Google have lots of free tools to tell it all about your business. You'll need to open a Google account. You can then submit your website to it for indexing. Until is indexed by google it won't appear in search results. Depending on your timing with regards to opening you can pay to accelerate the process. You'll also want to add your shop to Google Places for Google Maps inclusion.

For general chocolate searches you'll probably show up on page 900 to start with, but as Google is now much more mobile and local focussed, someone searching for a chocolate shop in your area may well be presented with your shop once Google has verified you are a genuine business at that location.

Google now uses a couple of hundred signals to determine how it displays you so avoid paying for Search Engine Optimisation (SEO). The main thing that will get your site visible is relevant content – so start writing about your shop on your website, and build reference links from trusted sources that are built organically over time (a reference link is another website linking to yours). You might want to join the local Chamber of Commerce and get listed on their site with a link to yours for example. But avoid trying to overly jump start your site, it will take time and many visitors will come to your site once they have found you through your physical shop. Put your website domain so it's easily seen by your shop customers, perhaps on receipts or on gift tags.

Press Releases

A good way to kick your shop launch off is to get yourself in the local paper by sending out a press release for your shop launch.

Firstly you can start to make yourself a Press Release email list by researching local papers and magazines and noting the various content editors emails and names. I know lot's of people hire PRs to do this and get good results, but we've always done this ourselves and managed to get good coverage. Every pound you give to someone else you'll have to earn back as profit!

Now you need to put together a Press release – there are lots of template examples you can google for this, but generally they take the form something like below.

_____

Press Release

My Town, My Shire, Immediate release

My Chocolate Shop opens in My Town

95

A new chocolate shop opens in My Town this Saturday 20th November. The chocolate shop named My Chocolate Shop is run by Walter White and family. The shop will sell a range of artisan chocolates from local and award winning chocolatiers and a range of chocolate bars and gifts.

Owner Walter White says "We're so excite to be opening in My Town, it's been a life long dream to run a chocolate shop"

The new shop has a website MyChocolateShop.co.uk and Mr White plans to sell online in the near future so tourists that visit can continue to buy My Chocolate Shop chocolates.

About My Chocolate Shop

My Chocolate Shop opens Saturday 20th November at 1 Chocolate Arcade, My Town.

Business owners: Walter White

Website: www.mychocolateshop.co.uk telephone 12345

Hi Resolution Press resolution images are available to download on Dropbox here....

_____

Once you have drafted a short press release you'll need to send it to your list. Initially your list might be quite small and you can send it using a normal email package. But beware your email host will have a limit on the number of emails you can send per hour. You can also get your email blacklisted sending unsolicited emails.

For this reason in the long run you'll want to use a newsletter package to send your Press Release and ultimately other newsletters.

One solution is Mail Chimp or it's equivalent. For Wordpress users Mail Poet is very good. It's worth paying for these packages as they make sending newsletters so much easier. They are experts at getting mail delivered and avoid you being blacklisted as a spammer. Mail Poet is integrated as a Wordpress plugin so if you use Wordpress you can save effort by writing your press release as a website post then send it via Mail Poet.

Hopefully the press will be interested and at the thought of a box of chocolates for the office will send a photographer around.

I mentioned newsletters. Once you are open you should start to gather customers names and emails (with their permission!). You should also try to create separate lists. For example one list for customers that live in My Town, one for the Press, one for trade customers. You can then send newsletters to specific groups – a tasting evening might only be of interest to residents of My Town for example. If you have a website sign up it can automatically add the names to your lists.

SOCIAL MEDIA

There's no escaping social media. At the very least you should open an account in your shop name, or as close to it as you can and put up a holding page with opening hours and a few photographs. Consider Facebook, Twitter, Instagram, Google Plus (mainly because it's google even though nobody really uses it), and You Tube.

Personally I would avoid paying other people to do your social media – it's free, and it's you your customers want to connect with. As a small business owner one of your most powerful assets on social media is people can connect with you the owner. But it takes time and can prevent you ever switching off from work. It's possible to spend hours on Facebook or twitter but if used well it can be a powerful selling tool.

Look at @AlyssaJewellery on twitter who has built a jewellery business almost entirely on twitter followers. Sticky Walnut @StickyWalnut are the other spectrum of how to be incredibly funny and extremely rude on twitter and make it work for them.

We ourselves won former Dragon's Den star The Paphitis' SBS award – a twitter competition he runs each week. We attended an awards ceremony, had a photograph with Theo and got into the local papers. So social media can help.

29: With Dragon's Den star Theo Paphitis

TRIP ADVISOR

Trip advisor can be a bit of a double edged sword. My advice would be to avoid gathering reviews until you're sure of your continued good customer service. You may not be able to avoid it of course. If you give excellent customer service you should be fine!

CUSTOMER SERVICE

It doesn't matter how good your shop fit is or how wonderful your products are, if your customer service is poor you'll rapidly lose customers and find it hard to get them back!

But it's not Rocket Science. Be nice to people and if something goes wrong put it right straight away. In difficult situations stay calm and don't argue with the customer. Think of it from their point of view, usually they have a problem that needs solving and the quickest way to diffuse a situation is to put the problem right.

We've often found that harder to put right situations occur when something hasn't met someone's expectations. As an artisan people will often buy a gift from you to impress someone or show that they have put some thought into their gift. If the recipient isn't suitably delighted (for whatever reason) then you'll probably get the blame. As an online provider we also have what we call the 'forgot my mother's birthday' scenario. This takes the form of guilt transference where at 11:59 at night someone will order online for a birthday delivery the next day. If it doesn't get there of course it's your fault not theirs!

We managed to build an excellent reputation for our own shop, gaining nothing but 5 star reviews and listings in Lonely Planet and Time Out Cotswolds as one of the best places to visit. Mostly this was achieved by working hard, providing excellent products and service, and being nice to people!

ACCOUNTS AND BOOK KEEPING

I have to admit I used to absolutely dread doing our accounts. I was using an accounts package called Sage Instant Accounts at the time. It would take me hours to work through shop receipts, invoices and try and reconcile everything. I had a big briefcase full of paperwork we fondly referred to as the 'box of doom'! However I did recognise how important it was as if you don't keep your accounts up together you have no idea if you're being a busy fool, or even worse losing money for some reason, be it shop lifting or the unthinkable, through a member of staff!

Accounting became a lot easier when I moved to the cloud a couple of years ago and an accounts package named Xero. The great thing about Xero is it integrates with lots of other packages. So I use a utility called Receipt bank that lets me email or photograph invoices and receipts and it strips out the relevant information and forwards it to Xero, a bit like an automated book keeper. My Bank account automatically feeds into Xero as does Paypal and also my online orders through a website plugin. Life is now so much easier!

I'd certainly recommend Xero and Receipt Bank in combination (I don't get money for this referral I just think they're worth the monthly fee for the time saving).

Banking takings from your shop daily will help you reconcile your till takings. Reconcile essentially means making sure that what the till says matches your bank deposits.

You could of course hire a book keeper and present them with all your receipts and I know many people who do this. Personally I prefer to keep on top the accounts myself and view Receipt Bank as my bookkeeper.

STOCK TAKES

Stock takes are another send you to sleep task, but they are so important. A daily or weekly stock take is also important to allow you to restock. Depending how big your shop is and how many units you sell (SKU) this could be a simple spreadsheet with a look around the shop, counting and filling in the sheet in between customers. You may want to set a minimum amount for each stock item and deduct your stock from the minimum holding level to work out the reorder quantity. Most big stores automate this process.

Ok, so your till reconciles against your bank takings, but that doesn't mean that you aren't losing money. The only way you prove this is to do regular stock takes and cross check that the difference in stock between stock takes matches what your accounts say you've sold.

If the stock take says you've sold more stock then the accounts package then either...

- You've miscounted stock

- Some stock has gone missing

- Not all of your takings have gone through the till or an error has been made entering sales

We've had all of these instances when running shops and market stalls. When we're running busy market stalls we count stock in each morning and out each night much to the amusement of our fellow traders. But it means we know exactly how much we've sold for restocking, and also whether all cash is accounted for. We've had instances where the cash is significantly out and found a roll of notes fallen behind the counter for example.

It's also important to let your staff know that you're performing stock takes and reconciling till takings. I'm sure you've seen those secret camera shows where an owner suspects a member of staff of stealing. When confronted the member of staff will deny everything. Unfortunately almost all businesses will experience this at some point. We certainly have! It's horrible when it happens and leaves you feeling sick. It also destroys trust.

The best way to be prepared for this is to have procedures in place for stock takes and till reconciliation such that you spot discrepancies quickly and pick up on them. If takings seem unusually low switch your working day to see if things are that quiet when you work? Perhaps use a secret shopper.

If you notice that card takings are unusually low in proportion to cash on a certain shift this can also be a warning sign.

Most importantly be careful of accusing staff and don't follow your prejudices. Go on evidence and if money does go missing daily banking will help identify when it potentially happened.

Shoplifting and Other Scams

SHOPLIFTING

At some point you'll experience shop lifting, though it's not always easy to spot. At one point our shop manager suspected that a young after school visitor was helping herself. We installed a parabolic mirror and she was spotted putting chocolates into her bag behind our central display unit. But it was only when we put the mirror up we were able to see her.

We contemplated CCTV but as such a small shop it seemed that it would be intrusive on our customers and perhaps also send a message to our staff that we didn't trust them.

OTHER SCAMS

There are several scams that you may experience. One that pops up every now and again is the change of £20 note. A customer will buy a small item, say a lolly, and give you a £20 note. As you go to give them change they'll stop you and say no wait and they'll give you something smaller and ask for the twenty back. They'll attempt to fluster you and you'll end up giving them the £20, change and the goods before you realise it.

When working in large cash situations we usually put the customers note in a completely separate place whilst giving change to avoid it. One of our shop assistants even got into the paper catching out a gang who tried to pull this trick on us twice!

KEEPING IT ALL GOING

So that's it, congratulations - you're a bona fide Chocolate Shop owner running your own business!

Remember to sit back and look at your accounts every couple of months to see if you're where you think you should be. Above all don't be complacent and think – it's my first year, we'll see how it goes. Plot your sales against our graph showing seasonal trends – what does the yearly average look like, are you on track?

Keep an eye on cash, so many businesses fail as they run out of cash. You'll be cash rich after Christmas and Easter, but this will need to carry you through the leaner months.

Every now and then stand outside your shop and look at it as if from a new pair of eyes – does it look good, does your signage make sense? Walk in to your shop... are your signs correctly placed, does the stock look good, are the shelves dusty? It's easy to miss things when you're caught up in the day to day.

Remember to take some time off too and forget about work. This will actually help look at day to day issues with new perspectives.

Take a review each year – January is a good time for this. Are you achieving your goals, is the business working for you, do you need to change anything?

Above all remember to enjoy life and being master of your own destiny!

SELLING YOUR BUSINESS

Though this might seem a long way a way at some point you might decide to sell your business. We've had some experience of this and there are a few pitfalls to avoid.

There are lots of sales agents out there who will want to sell your business. It's worth talking to them and getting their valuation. But beware they don't really care about your business, just their percentage. Consequently many will give you an unrealistically high valuation. They take a few photographs and list you on the usual businesses for sale website. You can spot the listings – high valuations, almost no photographs or information and a contact the agent number. You will still need to pay a solicitor to do the legal part.

When we sold our shop business we got three vastly different valuations and then picked one our self that we felt was justifiable and would also lead to a sale within six months. We paid for a three month listing on businesses for sale and put on lots of excellent photographs, financial information, inventory and reasons to buy. Within a month we had three viable offers and one at the asking price. We accepted and completed the sale within five months of advertising the business.

If you have time to wait then you can try a higher price, but it's very hard to keep a business sale quiet and it may affect your shop staff and customers.

Appendix 1 – Business Plan Template

The Template below can be used as a basis for your own business plan. It's based on the one we used to open our shop that was described by several bank managers as the best they'd ever seen – usually followed by a polite decline to loan money! But don't be deterred, putting your ideas on paper in a structured form will help you clarify your plans and make them seem more real.

The plan uses generic names such as 'My Chocolate Shop', My Town etc

My Chocolate Shop

Business Plan

Author Walter White

Executive Summary

My Chocolate Shop is a Luxury chocolate shop and cafe based in My Town.

Founded in *month/year* this business plan will demonstrate how My Chocolate Shop will develop a successful and profitable chocolate shop in My Town.

Table of Contents

Fill in your table of contents here

Business Description – My Chocolate Shop

Introduction

My Chocolate Shop is a MyTown based retailer of Luxury handmade chocolates.

Our mission is:

"To become the destination for a unique chocolate gift".

My Chocolate Shop was founded in *month / year* by *your name*. Describe your background and your background to opening your Chocolate Shop.

Briefly describe your shop location.

The diagram below illustrates our vision of ours business structure in five years time. Draw a diagram of how your business might look in five years time. Will there be more than one shop?

Our Products

Describe the products you want to sell, unique selling point, possible partnerships with suppliers.

Positioning

Chocolates

The luxury chocolate market in the UK is highly competitive.

It broadly divides into cheap mass produced confectionery, medium quality mass produced chocolates, and artisan handmade chocolates. More recently Bean to Bar makers and Raw chocolate have also carved niches.

The mass produced confectionery producers are well known and established - Cadburys, Mars etc

The medium quality market is equally competitive. There are two large producers - Thorntons and Hotel Chocolat. We also consider that in our local sector x,y,and Z chocolates fall into this sector.

Pricing

Briefly describe your pricing strategy. If you are supplying luxury handmade chocolates you will be able to charge a premium price for quality.

Typically you should aim to make a 50% gross profit margin. This is sometimes referred to as Keystone pricing. Essentially with a keystone pricing model you double the cost price to create your retail selling price.

If you buy from a distributor they will add their own margin on top of the suppliers so you may need to opt for a smaller margin of 35% in order to sell at the manufacturers RRP. In the UK manufacturers can suggest retail prices but you are free by law to sell at any price you like. So in theory you could always make a 50% gross profit on every product. But it depends what you're selling, where else it is available and if your customer base is willing to pay that price for the product.

So forgetting about VAT for now, if a product is sold to you for £5, to make 50% margin you need to sell the product for £10.

Gross Margin % = (Retail selling Price – Wholesale price to you)/ Retail Selling Price x 100

Large luxury department stores typically aim to price at above the 50% margin rate. Discounters will price at much less than the rate aiming for a large turnover. So there is no hard and fast pricing rule but as you're unlikely to have bulk buying capability your purchasing and pricing should reflect your niche.

The Market

The UK confectionery market is expected to reach a value of £6.46bn by 2019 Chocolate confectionery accounts for nearly three-quarters of sales by value.

Premium chocolate represents a fast-growing and dynamic market, with global sales rising. Sales and consumer awareness are both growing for a variety of reasons – these include wider availability of premium chocolate at the retail level and high levels of new product activity. Additionally, more consumers are becoming attracted to dark chocolate on account of its health benefits, while ethical concerns have increased demand for organic and Fairtrade chocolate, all of which tend to be positioned at the premium end of the market.

Customers

Adapt this to suit your target demographic, for example...

My Chocolate Shop's target customer could possibly be best described as the Sunday Times or Country Living magazine reader. That is an affluent customer or chocolate connoisseur able to differentiate the quality of My Chocolate Shop's products.

Market Size/Trends

The UK market is becoming more sophisticated in terms of premium chocolate and is starting to differentiate fine chocolate in a similar manner to fine wines.

Mintel said that healthier dark chocolate sales continue to increase.

"Consumers are cutting back on their 'unhealthy' treats. Yet, when they do indulge, they often want the best."

My Chocolate Shop is planned to open in My Town.

My Town – Explain why My Town is a great location for your shop.

Competition

The luxury chocolate market in the UK is highly competitive. My Chocolate Shop competes with the premium quality chocolate retailers.

Local Retail Competition My Town location

Explain who your competitors are locally.

Regional Competition

Regionally My Chocolate Shop competes with the following chocolatiers in local independent outlets

Explain some of your regional competitors

National Competition

Describe some of the National competitors that might impinge on your success either by potential opening near you or selling online.

Estimated Sales

The following estimated sales are based on our best estimate of trading using sales patterns from a real chocolate business in a similar location to My Chocolate Shop.

It's very hard to estimate sales until you open but use our sales patterns to perform your best estimate based on your size of shop and potential footfall.

The spreadsheet below shows how you might estimate sales. The £150,000 is purely an example figure! The spreadsheet sets a target per year for the shop and then breaks that down into a daily target and how that might translate into sales, allowing you to see if such sales are realistic.

It's so easy to overestimate sales! Tweak the spreadsheet a little and you'll be calculating huge sales.

The biggest mistake we made when opening our first shop was to overestimate sales!

We also didn't realise just how much sales varied with seasons, pay day, the weather, special events.

But you can only take your best estimate. Stake out the area you plan to open over a number of days or weeks, count footfall. Sit in similar shops and cafes or discretely check out their accounts online. The more real life information you have the better. Look at businesses for sale online and obtain as much information on turnover as you can. Look at other shops in the same town you're looking at.

Café and Retail Sales

My Chocolate Shop chocolate shop have estimated sales as below. You can recreate a similar spreadsheet to experiment.

Target Per Annum(TA)	£150,000.00	
Weeks Open (A)	51.00	
Days per Week (B)	6.00	
Days Open (C= AxB)	306.00	
Target per Day (TD=TA/C)	£490.20	So this is the daily target. How might this break down?
Coffee		
Cost per Cup (Co)	£2.00	
Cake per slice (Ca)	£2.75	
Coffee per 10 people (CoN)	10	
Cake per10 people (CaN)	4	Assume 4 in 10 people have cake with coffee
Average sale per person (AvS)	£3.10	=((Co x CoN) + (Ca x CaN)) /10 = ((2 x 10) + (2.75 x 4))/10
Number of Stools	5	
Avg covers (AvCov)	3	
Total avg per hour (AvH)	£9.30	=AvCov x AvS Assumes 3 people per hour
Hours per day (h)	8	

111

Avg per day (AD)	£74.40	=h x AvH
Retail		
Total Coffee people per day (TCP)	24	=AvCov x h
Conversion to retail (conv)	10.00%	Assumes 10% of people having coffee also buy something
Avg Retail Spend (Ar)	£10.00	Assume £10 average retail spend
Retail from Coffee (RFC)	£24.00	= TCP x Ar x conv/100
Total from Café per year	£30202.20	= (AD + RFC) x C = (£74.70 + £24) x 306
Retail only shoppers per hour (Rn)	5	Assume 5 shoppers per hour just buying
Retail from shoppers (Rd)	£400.00	=RnxArxh =5 x £10 x 8
Total from Retail per year	£122,400	=RdxC =400 x 306
Total	£498.40	=£400 + £24 + £74.40
Total Turnover	£152,602.20	=£122,400 + £30,202.20

Thus total sales from the Café and retail are estimated at 152,602 per year.

For our first year this will be pro-rata dependent on target opening of the retail unit.

You can also use a spreadsheet like this to hypothesise. For example if your sales are low, how much difference would the up sell of a chocolate with coffee make? We used to offer this with the slightly cheekily named 'a bit on the side' – pay 60p and choose any chocolate to accompany your coffee. From the spreadsheet you can add a conversion rate, say 1 in 5 customers or 0.2 choose this option, multiply it up...

0.2 customers x 3 Avg Covers per hour x 8 hours x £0.6 x 306 days per year = £881 extra per year. Small differences like this can add up and often only require you or your staff to suggest "would you like to choose a chocolate with your drink for 60p?"

This spreadsheet doesn't include any Ice Cream sales but you could perform similar calculations to guess-timate how much Ice cream sales could add per year.

Chocolate Workshops

My Chocolate Shop plan to run chocolate tasting events and workshops.

Estimated income £3000 – for example.

Based on £25 per person per 2 hour workshop. 8 person per workshop - £200 per workshop. 15 events per year.

Fairs & Shows

MyChocolate Shop plans to promote and sell at the following local shows and events.

Total Sales £5000 – for example

Online

My Chocolate Shop plan to sell online and build a network of visitors to target for continued online sales.

Estimated sales £5000 for example

Sales Summary

Thus total estimated sales for the year xxxx are:

Online £5000

Retail & Café £152,000

Workshops £3000

Fairs & Shows £5000

Total Sales (Turnover) £165,000

This assumes a single retail unit.

Development and Production

Development Status

Describe how far you are with your plans...

My Chocolate Shop...

- Is registered with the Environmental Health Officer as a food retailer and had initial discussions
- Has trademark registered its name
- Has an extensive supplier network
- Has an Operations manual in progress to enable expansion of the business with replicable procedures
- Has a stock database in progress for supply chain management
- Is a member Taste of the West, The Guild of Fine Food and the Chamber of Commerce
- Undertakes ongoing marketing through local business group talks and social media
- Has a single page website

The Café retail unit potential location has been identified:-

no 1 My Town

Lease negotiations are under way. My Chocolate Shop expect to have the unit operational and open for business month/year.

Chocolate packaging

My Chocolate Shop has identified the following specialist chocolate packaging suppliers.

- Meridian Speciality Packaging
- Keylink
- My local printer

Expenses and Capital Requirements

Operating Expenses

The following provides an estimate of the Operating costs of the business. It includes fixed costs related to premises rental and running costs, website operation, membership fees and accountancy.

Retail Unit Fixed Costs

These are based on the My Town retail unit

Create your own spreadsheet with estimated costs.

Fixed Costs

Premises			
Rental	11000		
	11000	11000	
Rateable Value	11000		
Rates	5038		
Relief	0		
	5038	5038	
Service Charge	500		
Running Costs	2000	2000	

Insurance	400	400
Maintenance		200
TOTAL		18638

Capital Requirements

The following details the retail unit refit costs. Create your own spreadsheet based on your shop fit. We used a similar spreadsheet for our shop and managed to bring in the shop fit very close to our estimates.

Retail Space	Unit Cost	Qty
	Excl VAT	
Display		
Paneling	£19.12	4
Corners	£10.00	5
Shelf	£8.26	20
Gondola	£173.91	1
Pricing Gun	£26.09	2
Till&Barcode	£256.52	1
POS Software	£94.78	1
Chilled cabinet	£869.57	1
Coffee Shop		
Coffee Machine	£1,739.13	1
Counters	£3,695.65	1
Granite?	£1,739.13	1
Furniture		
Stools	£208.70	5
Tub Chairs	£286.96	0
Sofa	£434.78	0
Table tops	£39.13	0
Table Base Brushed Steel	£56.52	0
Chairs	£52.17	0
Crockery	£27.78	1

Crockery	£5.80	2
Cuttlery-knife	£5.95	2
cutlery-fork	£3.10	2
cutlery tea spoon	£2.94	2
Dishwash er Undercou nter	£747.83	1
Coffee Shop fixed installatio n		
Retail / coffee flooring	£1,739.13	0
Decoratio n	£434.78	0
Lighting	£869.57	0
Air Con	£1,304.35	0
Shop fitting Labour	£3,478.26	1

This list is by no means exhaustive. When setting up our shop we had decided to register for VAT in order to claim back VAT. Consult with an accountant on this, it *may* be possible to register for VAT some months after opening and back claim VAT on purchases.

Cost of Goods

My Chocolate Shop aims to make an average 50% gross margin on its sales.

For example if a chocolate bar costs £1 excluding VAT wholesale, My Chocolate Shop will retail at £2+VAT retail.

Sales and Marketing

Sales and Marketing Strategy

My Chocolate Shop will develop a successful sales and marketing strategy to differentiate the quality of their product.

MyChocolate Shops website acts as a virtual shop window.

117

The opening will be accompanied by a press release with the aim of gaining local press coverage building press contacts.

Attendance at selected fairs provides valuable customer contact and MyChocolate Shop will continue this strategy at selected events.

Website statistics and Google tools provide useful information on who is visiting the My Chocolate Shop website and what they are searching for. These tools will continue to be used to hone My Chocolate Shops website.

The launch of a Retail premises and café will be accompanied by publicity such as...

- A launch party inviting buyers, customers and press as well as family and friends
- Balloon release with a voucher attached
- Advertising in County magazines
- Tasters and fliers around My Town

Advertising and Promotion

My Chocolate Shop will use a variety of methods to publicise their products

- Online promotion through www.mychocolateshop.co.uk
- Directory Listings both online and paper
- Entry into retail award competitions and the resulting publicity
- Press releases and article writing
- some Branded packaging
- Attendance at local fairs and charity events
- Supply of chocolates for specific events
- Local Radio and television contacts
- Offering competition prizes (everyone loves chocolate!)
- Selective charity donations .
- Social Media

Management

Management Description

Describe your Management team background – this may just be yourself.

Draw a structure of how your shop team roles might look- buyer, barista, sales assistant. Then allocate those roles – they may be allocated all to yourself initially.

Most of the roles below might seem a bit 'big business' so feel free to prune them down to something more suitable to your shop.

Managing Director

Walter White

- Responsible to shareholders / owners
- Responsible for ensuring that the brand performs to the shareholders / owners expectations
- Key Strategic decisions

Sales & Marketing Director

May Sellalot

- Responsible to Managing Director & Shareholders
- Overseeing Website
- Advertising etc
- Market trends & competition
- Food shows
- Brand Identity
- New markets
- Market share

Accounts & Finance

Doreen Counter

- Responsible to Managing Director
- Responsible for paying bills, reconciling the daily accounts etc
- Submitting accounts to HMRC
- PAYE & NI
- Sick Pay etc
- Pension Schemes
- Accounts for inspection by Sales Director

Head of Buying & Packaging

Arthur Box

- Responsible to Sales Director
- Responsible for ordering/securing perishable items at best price
- Liaising on design / ordering of packaging
- New packaging development
- Ensuring quality control

Head of Operations & Human Resources

Walter White

- Responsible to Sales Director
- Responsible for support to Shop Managers with a view to achieving targets, identifying operational problems and assisting with recruitment, staffing issues, premises
- Customer service

Ownership

The company is of private Limited status and is jointly owned by Walter White and May Sellalot in a 50:50 share split.

Support Services

My Chocolate Shop uses Bean Counters Accountants for accountancy support and advice.

Taste of the West are a valuable resource for assistance and advice on food industry matters.

The Chamber of Commerce provides advice, support and access to training.

Financials

Risks

My Chocolate Shop have identified the following potential risks and a mitigation strategy.

Competitors cut prices

Though at the high quality end of the market My Chocolate Shop is not completely price immune.

There is competition from the Supermarkets and other local companies attempting to capitalise on the popularity of Luxury chocolate. My Chocolate Shop must therefore continue to innovate and stay one step ahead.

Key customers cancel contracts

My Chocolate Shop has tried to spread it's product portfolio through online, and shop sales to individuals such that it is not completely dependent on one customer.

Industry Growth Rate Drops

Though the popularity of chocolate shows no sign of abating markets can change. My Chocolate Shop may need to diversify its range if the market changes significantly.

Production Costs Increase

The recent turbulence in the exchange rate and the high price of chocolate in the commodities market may cause price increases.

In the worst case the global chocolate market may not be able to support future demand or may be affected by changes in global weather patterns.

In this extreme My Chocolate Shop would need to diversify it's product portfolio.

Sales projections are not achieved

The biggest risk is with the proposed retail and café outlet. In the first instance My Chocolate Shop will try everything possible to identify and increase retail and café sales. It may be possible to increase sales through outside events and local corporate ties.

Suppliers fail to deliver

My Chocolate Shop will aim to build good relationships with more than one key supplier.

Competitor Opens nearby

This is always a risk. My Chocolate Shop will aim to build a loyal customer base.

Public Opinion of My Chocolate Shop changes

The general public is notoriously fickle and it is possible that as My Chocolate Shop trades public opinion may change. My Chocolate Shop intends to employ local people through apprenticeship schemes. My Chocolate shop will engage with the local community and monitor social media and Trip Advisor reviews.

Health of Key employees

For the first year the success of the business will fall on the ability of the owner in particular to train people in the operation of the shop. The owner plans to document all operations, recipes and processes with the aim of making the first shop a replicable model.

Project Plan

You might want to use a free project planning tool to show the time scale and activities of your shop opening.

Cash Flow Statement

A Cash Flow statement is an important part of your plan and will help you work out how much cash you will need. You can also monitor your progress when you open.

The table below show the projected cash flow for the period April 2xxx to September 2xxx. You'll want to go at least a year but i've shortened it to keep the table on the page. The figures are fictional and in many cases you can only take your best guess. But at least if you put something down it will help you plan!

Your gross profit margin is typically 35% if you buy from a distributor to 50% if you buy direct from a supplier. Though it's not always this simple. For planning purposes you could estimate based on 50% margin. That is ignoring VAT for now, if you sell a product for £10, at 50% margin the cost of the product to you is £5. This is sometimes referred to as Keystone pricing.

In the example below the shop starts with £5000 in the bank but after a busy April it dips before a small rally in the summer holidays. You need to plan for the whole year in a simple spreadsheet like this and continually update it. Almost all retail businesses rely on Christmas sales in December to make a profit and as a chocolate shop this will be amplified. Easter will be your second biggest sales period.

Cash Flow Statement	2xxx					
	Apr	May	Jun	Jul	Aug	Sep
Sales Online	£500.00	£400.00	£200.00	£100.00	£100.00	£200.00
Sales local corporate	£250.00	£200.00	£200.00	£200.00	£200.00	£200.00
Sales Retail	£8,000.00	£5,000.00	£5,000.00	£5,500.00	£7,000.00	£5,000.00
Sales Cakes	£500.00	£500.00	£500.00	£500.00	£1,000.00	£500.00
Sales Workshop	£500.00	£0.00	£0.00	£0.00	£500.00	£0.00
Sales Fairs & Shows	£1,000.00	£0.00	£0.00	£0.00	£0.00	£0.00
Total Sales	£10,750.00	£6,100.00	£5,900.00	£6,300.00	£8,800.00	£5,900.00
Cost of Sales Online	£250.00	£200.00	£100.00	£50.00	£50.00	£100.00
Cost of Sales Corporate	£125.00	£100.00	£100.00	£100.00	£100.00	£100.00
Cost of Sales Retail	£4,000.00	£2,500.00	£2,500.00	£2,750.00	£3,500.00	£2,500.00
Cost of Sales Cakes	£250.00	£250.00	£250.00	£250.00	£500.00	£100.00
Cost of Sales Workshop	£250.00	£0.00	£0.00	£0.00	£250.00	£0.00
Cost of Sales fairs & shows	£500.00	£0.00	£0.00	£0.00	£0.00	£0.00
Cost of Sales Packaging Purchase	£500.00	£501.00	£502.00	£503.00	£504.00	£505.00
Total Cost of Sales	£5,875.00	£3,551.00	£3,452.00	£3,653.00	£4,904.00	£3,305.00
Gross Profit (Sales - Cost)	£4,875.00	£2,549.00	£2,448.00	£2,647.00	£3,896.00	£2,595.00
Overheads						
Telephone and Broadband	£60.00	£60.00	£60.00	£60.00	£60.00	£60.00
Shop Rent	£1,000.00	£1,000.00	£1,000.00	£1,000.00	£1,000.00	£1,000.00
Rates	£200.00	£200.00	£200.00	£200.00	£200.00	£200.00
Electricity	£100.00	£100.00	£100.00	£100.00	£100.00	£100.00
Water	50	50	50	50	50	50
Insurance	100	100	100	100	100	100
Service Charge	90	90	90	90	90	90
Wages	2000	2000	2000	2000	2000	2000
Total Overheads	£3,600.00	£3,600.00	£3,600.00	£3,600.00	£3,600.00	£3,600.00
Net Profit (Gross Profit - overheads)	£1,275.00	-£1,051.00	-£1,152.00	-£953.00	£296.00	-£1,005.00
Cash in Bank	5000 £6,275.00	£5,224.00	£4,072.00	£3,119.00	£3,415.00	£2,410.00

Appendix 2 – What is chocolate?

Before we jump into the business side of things a brief background on chocolate is helpful.

Chocolate is made from the beans of the Cocoa Tree- more correctly know as Theobroma Cacao. Theobroma Cacao naturally grows in a narrow geographic band centred around the equator where climatic conditions suit. It originated in Central America and was later transferred to other growing regions as the Spanish, English and Portuguese brought cocoa to Europe. Thus cocoa plantations were developed in Africa – Ghana and the Ivory Coast, Madagascar, and the Caribbean islands.

30: Brightly coloured cocoa pods are the fruit of the Theobroma Cacao tree

Cocoa beans are really the seeds of the Theobroma Cacao tree and they reside in the centre of brightly coloured cocoa pods that are the fruit of the tree. When ready to harvest the pods are cut from the tree and the pods opened with a machete. The beans are scraped from the pod and the pod itself is discarded, though the white fleshy pulp is delicious.

31: *Cocoa Farmer and cooperative owner Monsieur Rene Julien demonstrates the opening of a cocoa pod*

The beans are taken by the cocoa farmers to a central area where they are put into fermentation boxes and covered with banana leaves. The beans spend around a week in the fermentation boxes and are regularly turned and moved through a set of boxes at different stages of fermentation. Fermentation is critical to remove the acidity in the bean.

After fermentation they are dried in the sun on large wheeled racks that can be put undercover if a rain shower occurs. At this stage the beans can be ruined if too wet and become mouldy.

Finally at this stage the beans are manually sorted into size groupings with the removal of any stray material.

The variety of the bean, the terroir of the growing region and the fermentation and drying process can all have a critical effect on the taste of chocolate.

The original South American varieties of bean are broadly classed as Criollo (cre-o-yo). These currently make up around 5% of the worlds chocolate. They are a delicate bean that is often white inside when the fresh bean is cut in half (not to be confused with the pod colour). Criollo beans are considered the holy-Grail to many chocolate makers and chocolatiers but in reality there are few genetically pure Criollo trees.

32: Madagscan Trinitario variety - the violet beans are forastero, the white are Criollo

Around 85% of the World's chocolate is made from the hardy Forastero variety. This disease resistant variety is common in the harsher growing regions of Ghana and the Ivory Coast where much of the world's bulk cocoa is grown. Known for a short flavour hit but lack of complexity this is the variety used by Cadburys, Mars, Nestle and most of the World's mass produced bars. Forastero beans are typically, but not always, purple when the fresh bean is cut in half (remember this is the bean centre not the pod colour). Again Terroir and genetic variations affect flavour and it would be unrepresentative to say that all Forastero beans are lower quality in flavour.

A third variety is the hybrid Trinitario variety. In regions such as Madagscar where both Criollo and Forastero trees have been planted a natural cross pollination has resulted in a hybrid where pods can contain both Forastero and Criollo beans. The fertile soil of Madagscar and terroir of the Sambirano Valley region has led to a complex fruity flavoured bean considered amongst the finest in the World.

There are of course many subtle genetic sub varieties, and like fine wines the beauty of chocolate is that beans grown in one region of the world can taste very different from those grown in another.

The dried and sorted beans are then transferred to a factory for further processing. In a few cases this is in the country of origin and this is the method we personally prefer as it keeps more money and skills within that country. It is sometimes referred to as Raisetrade or Equitrade and more recently Tree-to-bar. However most processing is performed in European and North American factories. You'll often hear people refer to Belgian chocolate – well they don't grow cocoa beans in Belgium!

Illustration

33: Chocolate Madagscar is wholly Malagasy family owned

In the factory the beans are carefully roasted*. The roasting of the beans again can greatly affect the finished taste of the chocolate.

*So called RAW chocolate omits this stage.

After roasting the beans are cracked into pieces called cocoa nibs, and then winnowed. Winnowing essentially blows air over the cracked nibs as they fall to remove unwanted thin pieces of the shell of the bean whilst the heavier cracked nibs drop into a collector.

The nibs are then taken through successive grinding stages in a melange or conch. As the nibs are ground to a fine paste sugar, milk powder, vanilla, and extra cocoa butter may all be added affecting the finished composition and flavour of the chocolate. An emulsifier is often used such as soya lecithin. The conching process lasts for typically 24 hours.

No milk powder is added for dark chocolate. Extra cocoa butter is sometimes added for a different texture. The more cocoa butter the smoother the texture. Sugar is often added for sweetness. So for example when you see a dark chocolate declared as 75% cocoa this will refer to the combined cocoa mass and cocoa butter. The remaining 25% will mostly consist of sugar and a fraction of a % may be the emulsifier. In order to compare the cocoa butter content of different dark chocolates you would need to examine the nutritional fat content as cocoa butter is the fat part of the bean. If two dark chocolate bars have the same 75% cocoa declaration but one has a much higher fat content then it is likely the cocoa butter to cocoa mass ratio is higher.

Milk chocolate has dried milk powder added. So a 40% cocoa milk chocolate will consist of 40% cocoa solids, again made up of cocoa mass and cocoa butter; typically 25% milk solids (this should also be declared), and 35% sugar. So Milk chocolate is usually, but not always sweeter. For example a Chocolat Madagscar milk chocolate is likely to have less sugar than a Cadbury's Bournville dark chocolate bar.

White chocolate has no cocoa mass only cocoa butter, milk and sugar. Typically white chocolate has the lowest cocoa % typically 30% and will consequently have the highest sugar content and is much sweeter.

After conching the chocolate is tempered. Chocolate in its natural state will solidify and form a number of different unstable crystalline structures. It is the beta crystalline structure that gives the snap and shine to chocolate. So the chocolate is heated to around 46 degrees C melting out all of the crystals. It is then cooled to a working temperature of around 30 degrees C whilst moving and seeding with chocolate of the desired beta crystal structure. The chocolate is then ready for use in moulding, enrobing, making bars etc.

34: a trio of tempering machines at Lick the Spoon UK

Chocolate that has been incorrectly tempered or is subject to heat can form unstable crystalline structures most commonly seen as a migration of cocoa butter to the surface giving a white bloom. Perfectly safe to eat but not desired and the bane of chocolatiers every where!

Similarly if subjected to moisture sugar can migrate to the surface forming a sugar bloom.

There are many more detailed books on the growing of cocoa and manufacture of chocolate but this crash introduction should help. As you can see there are many stages to creating chocolate and chocolates.

Appendix 3 - A BRIEF HISTORY OF CHOCOLATE SHOPS

In the UK confectionery was first introduced in the Tudor period. Confectioners at this time were valued as highly skilled artisans. Cocoa was introduced to the UK towards the end of the Tudor period, but it was in Georgian times that it started to gain popularity through companies such as Frys, Cadburys and Rowntrees.

Filled chocolates as we know them originated in continental Europe in France, Belgium and Switzerland. You'll encounter some common terminology amongst chocolatiers as particular centres have become so popular they are now commonly made by all.

Here are some common centres...

- Ganache – Usually a combination of chocolate and cream combined together to form a centre. A few chocolatiers have replaced the cream with water, so called water ganaches. Others have used coconut oil for a dairy free centre. Shelf life is affected by available water content so glucose is sometimes used or other additives that reduce available water content. So very long shelf life ganaches of supermarket chocolates can often be a trade off for a very sweet centre, low in cream and high in glucose.

- Praline – A nut based centre that can range from the very smooth to a more nutty texture.

- Rocher – French for rock – toasted nuts covered in chocolate.

- Truffle – a ganache based centre often round or piped and rolled in cocoa powder or icing sugar. As with moulded ganaches truffles can vary hugely from the traditional cream and chocolate ganache centre to very long shelf life centres with palm oil and vegetable fats which aren't really traditional truffles at all. In some countries like Germany the name Truffle is designated to a confection made solely of cream and chocolate with flavours and cannot be used if vegetable fats etc are used to replace the chocolate content. We often encountered people who 'didn't like truffles' and would choose our moulded ganache centres even though they were essentially the same thing in a different form. But they were basing their experiences on cheap supermarket truffles that tasted like margarine.

- Mendiants – A circular disk of chocolate topped with roasted nuts and fruits.

- Fondant creams – a traditional sweeter chocolate made with a soft sugar fondant centre for example Rose and Violet creams.

The kind of chocolate shop we think of from the book and film Chocolat really originated in France and Belgium and are still a joy to visit in many French towns today as the tradition continues. In the UK until around 20 years ago Thorntons was the closest UK equivalent and most people weren't familiar enough to notice the difference!

Over the last 20 years an explosion of Chocolatiers has occurred with Hotel Chocolat competing with Thorntons and very much improving the expected standard. In London alone there are several competing artisan chocolatiers and the UK is now producing chocolates equal to the finest in the world, often without the constraints of tradition allowing greater experimentation. This might be your journey!

Appendix 4 - SETTING UP A FRESH CHOCOLATE COUNTER

A choose your own fresh chocolate counter can offer your shop a fantastic visual showcase and unique selling point. But it is possible to get it wrong, so here's how we did it and also what not to do!

People will rarely tell you what they really think when they walk into your shop, but their eyes pick out things in minute detail, or at least mine do! So it's absolutely essential that your fresh chocolate counter knocks them smack between the eyes as the most beautifully presented, cleanest, mouth watering feast they've ever seen!

We recently made a family cycle ride to a nearby small town. We were tired and wet by time we got there and consequently feeling a bit dishevelled visited a small café and bakery that we hadn't been before. As we sat drinking our coffee I looked closer at the chocolates sitting in the glass counter. Now I know we are biased, but I doubt if they sold any – ever. They were of the mass produced Belgian variety, but in itself that potentially hit the right lower price point for the town. The main issue was their appearance. They were dusty, there were bits of cake crumbs that had dropped down from the cakes above that must have sat there for weeks. They were jumbled, poorly lit and didn't look appetising at all. To cap it all, though they were separated by a screen, they were sat next to a similarly sad looking selection of beige pies and sausage rolls.

35: *A beautifully presented fresh chocolate counter. You can clearly see the two layers separated by acrylic sheets.*

When you're running a shop and it's quiet it can be really hard to motivate yourself. People often thrive on the excitement of running a busy job and then lethargy sets in during the quiet periods. But that's the time to clean and rearrange your display such that when the next customer does walk in they're amazed by your selection. The marble slabs should be gleaming, acrylic sheets almost invisible and chocolates beautifully arranged – crumb, dust and bloom free.

We've already mentioned that we had a custom chocolate counter created in a dark wood veneer with the counter being open to selection by the public. But whatever counter you choose if you display the chocolates in right way people will only notice the overall effect. We've run fresh chocolate counters in two pop-up shops in Bath using the counters left in place by the previous owner. To display the chocolates we used £1 photo frames with glass we could clean. Perfect and low cost for a short term pop-up.

36: A low cost fresh chocolate counter for a pop up shop

For our Cirencester shop we had 20cm x 20cm marble slabs cut and polished at the same time we had the table tops made. These beautifully offset the dark counter.

On another counter we set up in a farm shop we used off the shelf slate tiles from the local DIY store that matched their more organic shop look.

The crucial bit is the next step. We had two clear acrylic sheets cut for each of the slabs. The chocolates sit on the acrylic sheets meaning the underlying slab doesn't get dirty and the chocolates can be displayed in two layers. The upper layer has the shortest best before date chocolates and this is the one the customer chooses from first. As the sheet is clear as the upper chocolates are removed the lower layer shows through giving the visual impression of an always full counter. Nobody wants to buy the last lone chocolate!

When the top layer is emptied the sheet can be cleaned, replenished and replaced as the bottom layer moving the bottom layer to the top. In this way the stock is rotated. With Lick the Spoon's wholesale chocolates we supply a small shouter with each order that displays the type of chocolate to the front and any allergens, and the best before date at the rear. Thus you always know the batch date of chocolates you are selling. We've had one local stockist telling us how having this information to hand on our chocolates helped her pass a spot EHO inspection.

It's important to clean the acrylic sheets regularly such that they always look spotlessly clean. We used to make the counter replenishment one of the first jobs in the morning before the shop got busy, or last thing on a Friday before a busy Saturday.

Another important aspect of our counter layout was the ability of the customer to be able to pick their own selection. Whilst we had a small sneeze screen and the counter had a deep lip, it was essentially open to the public. Whilst we had to debate this point with the local EHO, it really helped us to keep the counter moving with minimal staff during busy times. Initially we placed tongs and plates next to the till, though we soon realised it made more sense to have them at the far end near the entrance with the destination being the till.

37: Truffles can be better displayed in bowls

At the far end we had a simple pricing sign showing four different box sizes – 6, 12, 24, 48 and a loose per bag weight. Customers would pick a plate and tongues and choose their selection. Often of course they wanted guidance and this could be offered – it's part of the specialist shop service. But on busy Saturdays regulars could pick their selection without waiting to be served. In the run up to busy impulse occasions such as Valentine's we would pre-pack some boxes to speed things up.

You could of course offer gift wrapping if you have the space.

Our shop was small so we tended to use flat pack boxes supplemented with a few seasonal specials.

There is potentially more profit to be made with a fresh chocolate counter than with pre-packaged goods. The reason is when a manufacturer prices for a pre-packaged box they will need to include the labour cost in their pricing. If you pack your own boxes or even better have your customers pick their selection then this part of the cost is effectively absorbed in your shop running costs.

Some UK suppliers to help you supply your counter...

- Fresh chocolates - Lick the Spoon. Other suppliers are available, but it is our book! Chocolates are supplied in trays in square boxes to be decanted to your counter. Each variety comes with a small shouter showing awards won, allergens and best before date. The box itself contains full ingredients information.

- Chocolate Boxes - Meridian Speciality Packaging - A Worcestershire based company with a variety of off the shelf chocolate packaging available in small pack sizes of 25. They also offer the possibility of your logo on a box for as few as 100 boxes.

- Keylink.org A company with a variety of chocolate and confectionery packaging including bags, boxes, ribbons and bows. They too offer low volume bespoke printed boxes.

For a small first shop we would generally recommend off the shelf packaging customised either with for blocking or a ribbon and tag printed by your local printer.

Appendix 5 - SPECIALIST BEAN TO BAR CHOCOLATE

We talked earlier about the possibility of including specialist 'bean to bar' or 'tree to bar' chocolate in your product mix. You could even purchase a small grinder for some retail theatre!

Of course in reality all chocolate is bean-to-bar it's really the scale of the producer here. The movement has been kick-started by the ready availability of small grinders supplied by companies such as Bean to Bar UK a subsidiary of the excellent HB ingredients. A small grinder can be purchased from as little as £150 and pre-roasted cocoa nibs can also be purchased for those that want to bypass roasting and winnowing.

Whilst in our opinion it is difficult to make a profit with such small scale processes it is a potential opportunity for retail theatre with perhaps some small scale chocolate making or demonstrations or courses. However be aware that most retail insurance policies don't cover such manufacturing or unattended machinery running.

By their very nature small scale makers aren't in a position to supply supermarkets and in most cases it would negate their ethics. So there is the opportunity to partner with small scale makers offering them a retail outlet and providing a unique point of difference to your offering.

One advantage of the Bean to Bar market is it has pushed the ceiling price of a Craft Chocolate bar much higher than previously possible with prices of £5-£10. It remains to be seen whether the general public will embrace these prices but as a specialist shop it's certainly worth testing the market. For our part as a manufacturer we have chosen to offer a compact range of interesting flavour bars that we know sell well with a single bean to bar offering of our Bronde bar.

It's an interesting and growing market but we predict that many of the current small scale makers will disappear. Early UK adopters who have made a mark include Duffy Sheardown. Many cocoa growers that supply the artisan market are now starting to make their own bars in what must be the ultimate goal as it retains more money in the country of origin. Our friends Kim and Lylette Russell of Crayfish Bay are one such example. Their recent crowd funding campaign has allowed them to start producing their own chocolate using charcoal roasters at Crayfish Bay on the island of Grenada.

Even if you choose not to offer bean to bar you should be aware of the trend and as a specialist retailer the connection with cocoa farmers in different regions of the world.

Appendix 6 - RAW CHOCOLATE

When discussing potential product mixes we looked at the recent Raw food movement and within that 'raw chocolate'. Raw chocolate makers miss out the bean roasting process claiming that this removes nutrients from the finished chocolate.

As we said - our opinion on Raw chocolate is taste it, if you like it or more importantly think your customers will like it then consider it. Most of the Raw Chocolate we've tasted has a fudge like texture that you might expect if you compress raw ingredients together into a single lump without any further processing. It's not something we're overly keen on, but it is a trend.

We also believe that the health claims made by the Raw Chocolate movement should be treated with caution. The product labelling we've seen is often not in the correct legal format and the legally protected 'Organic' word is used incorrectly by makers who are not registered as Organic. It is illegal to use the word organic on packaging unless you are certified with one of the Organic certification bodies. This applies even if your ingredients are organic, the certification bodies prove the traceability.

Don't be confused by the Raw movements over-use of the term 'Cacao' in place of Cocoa. Cocoa is simply an Anglicised misspelling of the word Cacao when beans were first brought to Europe. Cocoa beans and Cacao beans are different names for the same thing. It is the processing of the beans that differs. The Raw Chocolate movement has adopted the use of the word Cacao as though it is somehow magically different from cocoa - this isn't true, it's marketing. It is only in the English language that this difference occurs.

So in summary Raw Chocolate is possibly worth a try, particularly during January when diets kick in. It depends if you have a health conscious customer base and how far the media continue to promote unsubstantiated health claims to the public.

Appendix 7 - PATISSERIE

When choosing your product mix you may wish to consider patisserie.

The big problem with Patisserie or indeed any fresh food, sandwiches etc., is wastage. As a shop if you aren't turning over cakes daily you'll need to throw them or give them away.

The way this is managed by stores such as Patisserie Valerie is to store as frozen and then put out to defrost in a chilled display cabinet. This way if you're careful you can reduce your deliveries and adjust your display to suit footfall patterns, more at weekends etc.

Unfortunately there are almost no high quality wholesale Patisserie suppliers in the UK and this is the main reason we didn't introduce such a counter.

Food to go is big business and one of the reasons why most Farm shops and Delis devote the majority of their space to a café. It's also the reason most of our high street has turned into coffee shops!

If you do find a suitable wholesale Patisserie supplier it's worth sourcing as beautiful a chilled display cabinet as you can afford and placing it in full view of the window with pricing so people can window shop and give them a reason to walk right in without the barrier of needing to ask price. But it is critical to keep that glass gleaming, the shelves spotless, and the display neatly arranged and enticing! Be prepared and budget for throwing or giving away unsold stock whilst you build your trade as you want people's experience to be of perfectly fresh items so they return. If your items are a little bit stale or not perfect people are often too polite or simply can be bothered to say, they just don't come back!

Appendix 8 - ICE CREAM

The natural counterpoint in your product mix to a hot sunny day is Ice Cream. Here are a few tips from our Ice cream experiences.

We switched Ice cream supplier a couple of times over the years of running our shop and perhaps came to a surprise conclusion regarding buying habits. Our shop was in a historic tourist town that attracted London visitors, but also many older visitors for a day out. We learnt that ...

- many people sought out very traditional flavours – mint choc, chip, vanilla, chocolate etc

- Whilst the Ice cream needed to be high quality, people didn't really appreciate the difference in the very highest quality we initially stocked and the more readily available organic Ice Cream we later stocked.

- The service level from the latter company was excellent and the ability to get emergency deliveries on weekends really helped us as the storage capacity underneath the freezer wasn't enough when the weather got really hot and we would sell out!

- People loved buying Ice creams in cones and there were few other shops offering this in town.

- People liked that the Ice cream was locally made

- We offered our own home made caramel sauce and served in higher quality waffle cones and these made a further point of difference.

We also developed a range of simple Ice cream sundae recipes to make further use of the Ice cream, though in our location nothing was as popular as a simple take away cone.

At one point we did enter into Ice Cream wars as nearby shops saw our popularity and decided they too would put in an Ice cream offering – there is no law against competition, be prepared for this! The sandwich shop next door put in a small slide top freezer and to our annoyance offered the same Ice cream brand as we did. Bad form on the Ice cream company we thought and told them so, but nothing we could do. However in our Ice cream 'Top Trumps' game a corner position and scoop top freezer offering a better visual display was more enticing than pre-packaged tubs and they eventually stopped selling and even offered us their freezer for sale!

A note on Environmental Health. Ice cream is a high risk product from an Environmental Health Point of view. It needs to be kept at the correct freezer temperature and you'll need a simple paper form to record your freezer temperature twice daily, you'll also need this for any fridges. You'll need a simple scoop and water jug for the scoop. The water jug will need to be cleaned and refilled several times a day with a small dash of food safe sterilising fluid such as Miltons fluid used for baby bottles.

You'll need to monitor delivery temperatures and keep hold of the delivery notes from your supplier. Ice cream cones will need to be kept in a clean dry place, off the floor.

You'll want to cover your scooping tubs at night with the lids provided.

If you don't have the space or simply can't afford it in your budget many Ice Cream companies will offer you a small slide top freezer providing you buy exclusively from them.

We found that in the winter months Ice cream sales would fall and maintaining the appearance of a scooping display became difficult without the turnover. We initially dropped the range of flavours offered and also switched to pre-packaged tubs that better suited the occasional winter buyer. You might event want to defrost and stop selling Ice cream in the winter months saving on electricity.

Appendix 9 - HOT CHOCOLATE

We used Italian style hot chocolate machines in our shop that contained a heat bain marie to keep the chocolate molten, and a rotating paddle to continuously mix the chocolate.

We made up our own hot chocolate recipe each morning using drops of chocolate and fresh milk. We would heat the milk in a jug using the steam wand of our coffee machine until steaming. We would then whisk in drops of chocolate whilst continuing to steam and whisk. The drops would not only melt into the milk, but by simmering and whisking would be emulsified in. Effectively forming a very milky ganache. Once fully whisked in we would pour it into the hot chocolate machine which would then keep it available for continuous use throughout the day.

- Advantages - hot chocolate continuously on tap for fast service during busy periods. Can also be used as a hot sauce for Ice Cream sundaes.

- Disadvantage - if you make too much you may need throw it away at the end of the day.

As the hot chocolate effectively forms a hot hold ganache we would reuse a fresh batch a maximum of two times by running off any unused hot chocolate each night into a jug, allowing to cool, then refrigerating over night. The next morning we would use the steam wand and whisk to reheat the hot chocolate. A paper record was kept each day so a maximum of two refrigerations were noted before throwing away. In busy times we would use all of the hot chocolate in a day or sometimes two batches.

As these machines run throughout the day cocoa butter can separate and form an oily looking film on the top of the chocolate. When cooled it looks like a white fat layer on top. Do not skim off and throw away this layer or you'll affect the composition of the chocolate. If it becomes too much of a problem choose a chocolate with a lower cocoa butter content. It can be heated and whisked back in.

Depending on your recipe the hot chocolate as it comes will make a rich 'intense' hot chocolate. Many customers will prefer a milkier hot chocolate. To achieve this steam more hot milk and add to the cup of intense hot chocolate. You can also use your imagination to create theatre with whipped cream and marshmallows.

As a specialist shop you might consider hot chocolates from different origins, a Madagascan and a Colombian for example. We added theatre by filling two grinders with different toppings – a chilli mix for an aztec hot chocolate and cinnamon, rose and cocoa nibs for a further variation. Bringing grinders to the table adds to the experience of visiting your shop.

For a small shop a limited menu is easiest. We offered an intense hot chocolate in an espresso cup with a home-made biscotti, a milky hot chocolate in a standard cup, and the ultimate rich hot chocolate with whipped cream, marshmallows and a hot chocolate spoon.

Your hot chocolate can also be used to make a mocha coffee.

We even tried using refrigerated hot chocolate in pastry cases as rich chocolate tart. Whilst the flavour was good it was a little messy for a small shop.

Top TIP: These machines have a removable top half for cleaning – if you lift them by this top half you will flood your shop with hot chocolate – I know, I've done this!

TIP 2: Use your hot chocolate as a hot Ice Cream sauce or to make a mocha coffee.

Appendix 10 – Till Systems

When you start looking at till systems there are a few arcane terms that you might come across. I'm not sure of the history behind these but they seem to be common terminology...

PLU – Price Look Up. Essentially a unique product identifier that can usually be given a text name and assigned a stock level (if used) a price and tax setting. For example PLU 1 might be allocated to a chocolate bar costing £3 at a tax rate of 20% i.e. standard UK VAT rate.

If you are planning to buy in products you will come across the concept of barcodes. Your till may have a barcode scanner (recommended) and in this instance your PLU will be the barcode. A note on barcodes in the next section.

You will want to allocate PLUs in your till for every item you sell in your shop including teas, coffees, cakes and other items that don't have a scannable code. For these you might want to either allocate a hot key on your till or a have a printed bar code on a sheet by the till that you can scan in. Either way you'll want to be able to quickly enter these items. Essentially any item that you sell that you might want to track should have a unique PLU in your till. These items will printed on the customer's receipt and any sales reports you print out.

- Cash / Card Sales – If you have a sophisticated till then your card machine may link to it and form part of the payment system. However it's more likely on a lower priced system that you'll have a completely separate card machine and use till buttons to identify card or cash payments.

- X Report – This is usually done at the end of the day when you're cashing up your till. It tells you the day's sales in cash and card to allow you to cross check. But importantly it doesn't zero the till's totals, so you can run this during the day to see how sales are doing.

- Z Report – the same as the X Report but zeros the till's totals ready for the next day. It's usually the last print out you do at the end of the day when you have cross checked your till totals.

Though this all sounds like some strange code language you'll soon get used to it and you too will be baffling people with talk of Z reports!

What are barcodes?

You'll no doubt have come across barcodes before but it helps to know a little more about them when setting up a shop. Most products you buy in will have a scannable barcode. This barcode is a unique identifier and in the UK is known as EAN or GTIN 13 format. Each barcode is unique and so the registration is managed centrally by an administration called GS1 who ensure each manufacturer has a unique barcode. Thus you can use a product barcode as a PLU in your till and be certain that it shouldn't clash with products from another manufacturer.

So what if you want to allocate and print your own barcodes? Well if it's purely for use in your own shop you can use any number you like so long as you can print it in a barcode format. There are free internet tools to convert numbers to printable barcodes. Though we were a manufacturer and had a GS1 license our shop was able to allocate PLUs for items such as Ice Cream etc., and these were often numbered 001, 002, 003...

If you reached the stage of wanting to sell to other stores it would need to be unique and require a license from GS1 at just over £100 per year for 1000 unique barcodes.

You may come across a longer barcode on the outer case of products. This is usually in GTIN 14 format and denotes a case quantity. It is essentially the unit bar code with an extra digit and checksum calculation.

Your chosen till should be able to scan GTIN-13 also historically known as EAN 13 barcodes. You can also get free smartphone apps which recognise barcodes.

Smaller suppliers may not have started to barcode their products. This isn't a problem in itself. But you will want to add a unique till PLU so you can track sales and also give an itemised receipt. We used a local fudge producer who didn't barcode their items so we used unique till PLUs for their products. Rather than scanning a barcode you manually enter the PLU to select the item. On a more sophisticated till it might be added as a hot key or selected on a touch screen menu.

I know that all sounds really complicated... essentially...

- Tills often term different products as PLUs- (Price Look Ups)

- Each product you sell should have a unique PLU to allow you to extract sales figures from your till, stock reports etc

- A manufacturer's barcode can be used as the PLU number

- A barcode scanner attached to a till allows you to scan the barcode, it's recognised as a PLU and the till looks up the price, tax etc.

- You'll still want to record sales of tea, coffee, cakes etc, but they won't be scannable. So you can either allocate a hot key that records their unique PLU, or have a barcode printed on a sheet next to the till

- You can allocate your own PLUs (and barcodes) for items in your shop, they're unlikely to clash with bought in items. To get a truly unique barcode you need to register with GS1 and pay an annual fee (not really needed in a small shop, just use 1,2,3 etc)

A quick note on Sales Tax - VAT

When you first set up your till you might not consider VAT if you think your turnover will be under the threshold. But you'll be entering tens to possibly hundreds of PLUs for all of the products you sell. If at this stage you enter them with the correct tax setting - say Tax 1 is VAT, but set the Tax 1 rate to zero%, then you'll be good to go if you register for VAT. Rather than changing hundreds of products you'll just need to change the Tax rate - well in theory! You may need to adjust for sensible pricing.

Similarly VAT in the UK is complicated regarding cakes and other items served in or to take out. Cakes sold to take away are currently zero rated for VAT. Cakes eaten in are considered a service and subject to VAT! So you'll need two Till buttons to track these sales. You will need to track them in case HMRC decide to audit you in five years time!

About the Author

Matthew Short is the Director of Lick the Spoon chocolates, a multi award winning UK based artisan chocolate company. The company was founded in 2006 by Matthew's wife and Creative Director Diana Short. Initially working from home they were named Best of Bakery and Confectionery at the Taste of the West awards in their first year of entering and were soon noticed on a national level. They were soon stocked by London department stores Selfridges, Harrods, Harvey Nichols, Liberty and John Lewis Oxford Street.

In 2009 as demand exceeded the capacity of their home kitchen, Matthew and Diana remortgaged their house put all of their money to set up from scratch a production facility – or 'chocolate factory' in Corsham, Wiltshire. At the same time they opened a beautiful chocolate shop in the historic Roman town of Cirencester, Gloucestershire. Over the next five years they won awards for their shop in Cirencester including the Small Business of the year award, and gained listings in Time Out Cotswolds and the Lonely Planet guide as the best places to eat.

Over the next ten years they opened several short let pop up shops in different towns and attended both regional and national food shows. They sold their Cirencester shop at a profit in 2014 to focus on their growing wholesale chocolate business. In 2016 they were named Supreme Champion at the Taste of the West awards, the first time in 25 years a chocolate company had won, and celebrated 10 years and over 60 fine food awards. They also for the first time followed the cocoa trail at its origins meeting the cocoa farmers and producers in Madagascar and Grenada.

A former engineer Matthew had early success as a schoolboy writing top 10 computer games in the early 1980s . He joined Rolls-Royce as an engineering apprentice winning the apprentice of the year award in his first year. After graduating with a first class honours degree in electronic engineering Matthew continued to work in engineering in a career spanning military electronics, to machinery design to telecommunications, working in several countries including the US, Germany, France, and Norway. A keen musician Matthew met wife

Diana whilst playing guitar in a jazz and blues band. In 2006 he left engineering to start their chocolate journey with Lick the Spoon.

Matthew and Diana live in Chippenham, Wiltshire with their two children.

Printed in Great Britain
by Amazon